# SANTA LOVES SNOWMEN

## Volume 24 by Jean Zawicki

**Every designer/author has those "SPECIAL PEOPLE" whose help and encouragement mean everything. Although I gratefully acknowledge a wonderfully loyal following of Santa lovers, I personally felt the stress last year producing yet another book! With the opening of the B & B along with a small gift shop that I try to fill with mostly painted pieces and painting supplies, I had decided that Heirloom Santas would be my last book for awhile.**

**One evening in early autumn, after a particularly busy summer, I went out to the shop workroom to do a few drawings for the first time since the '96 convention. I needed to do a few snowmen for a display for the shop's Christmas Open House in November.**
**At 1:00 a.m. there lay before me more than a dozen designs that had simply "rolled" off my pencil. There began my first doubts as to my "no more books" decision. I wondered if perhaps somebody up there was trying to tell me something, but I still wanted to stick by my original decision. I could always use the designs for convention in '97 and be way ahead for a change! I prayed for guidance, then proceeded to ask other painters what they thought of the designs.**

**During a couple seminars in Florida, I received LOTS of enthusiastic encouragement! I still wasn't convinced, then between the Florida seminars I woke one morning at 7:00 a.m. with the cover and the southern snowman design firmly in mind! Knowing how easily I can forget I dashed down to Mary Riley's studio, cup of coffee in hand and by the time Mary awoke, I had both designs ready to go.**
**At the Sea Oats seminar the following week-end, one of the girls had an idea for a design. To both our surprise, I had already drawn up my "Southbound Snowman" almost identical to what she envisioned. We had a good laugh, and that's "the rest of the story"!**

**Thank you all, from the bottom of my heart!**
**MAY GOD GUIDE YOUR BRUSH**

## PROJECT INDEX

I like to utilize the step-by-step pages rather than to repeat instructions for items that occur in more than one project. This allows more room patterns!


General Information . . . . . 2-5
Acrylic to Oil Conversion Page . . . . . 5
Santa Loves Snowmen (Cover) . . . . . 5- 6-7
Sassy Snow folks Cut-outs & Ornaments . . . 8-9
Mrs. Snowtapple Heart Plate. . . . . 10-11
Candle Follower & Photo Frame & Album . . . . 11
Winter With Feathered Friends . . . . . 12
Little Robin Red Breast & Santa on Heart . . . . 13
Step-by Step For Santa Face . . . . . 14-15
Step-by-Step for Snowmen & Misc. . . . . . 19
Sammy Snowman on a Chalk Board . . . . . 20
Holiday Tic-Tack-Toe Board . . . . . .21
Skating Snowman on multi-Point Quilt board . . 22
Snowman Centerpiece & Book Box . . . . . 23
Snow Angel . . . . . 24
Southbound - Southern Snowboy . . . . . 25
Santa Cookie Plate . . . . . 26-27
Misc., 4 Glass Balls & ornament reductions . . . 28
Strokework & accessory designs . . . . . 29
Ornaments, pins etc. . . . . . 30 -31
Small Plate border in gold . . . . . 32
General Information & Material Sources . . . . . 32


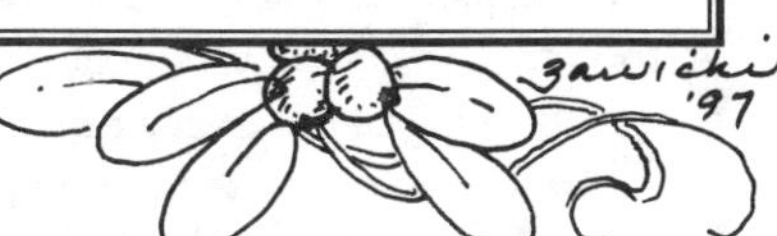




Disclaimer: The information in this book is presented in good faith. No warranty is given to the user relating to the material used in this book. Since we have no control over the physical conditions surrounding the application of the information contained herein, Jean Zawicki will not be liable for any untoward results, or charges made against the user for claims of patent or copyright infringement.



**Distributed by:** 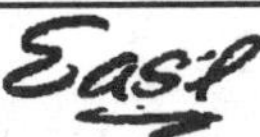

**Essential Authors Services Ltd.**
**P.O. Box 22088 • St. Louis, MO • 63126**
**Phone: (314) 892-9222**

# GENERAL INFORMATION

In general I sideload my brush to achieve a graduated "Floated Color" blend. I prefer the softness of several sheer layers of color rather than heavy opaque coverage that you must then struggle with it to make light and shadow show up. I utilize the background color as much as possible. Add more floated layers of medium to dark values in appropriate areas, then allow the light background to create a soft glowing (forward light) area. Lightly "Ghosting In" each area with floated color makes it easier to see and then intensify darker values with additional layers of color. Always blend out color toward the center in each area. NEVER allow color to flow all the way across the width of your brush, no matter how small the flat shader may be.

As a right handed person, I load my brush on the left or near side (reverse for lefties). The near side will always be the easiest side to see and control. I NEVER flip-flop my brush to load both top and bottom, or when applying the color onto the painting surface. Sometimes I get quite a bead of paint build-up on the top edge of the near side of the brush, but if you press the brush flat, firm and squarely as you load the brush for floated color, it will allow your paint to go a lot further before re-loading. Rather than to dip the corner of the brush into the paint and blend it into the brush in a separate area, I utilize my **PAINTER'S PAL Sta-Wet Palette**. I establish a blending path beside the paint pile and use this path for all my brush-loading, **cleaning it off** with a moist tissue **if the width of the blending path gets messy OR wider than the width of the brush being loaded.**

Place only a very **TINY DROP** of each color on the pre-soaked palette paper with each color family placed in a straight row ranging from light to darkest value. As a right hander, I blend into the upper right area of the color from 1-3 o'clock. Begin just outside the color, then stroke inward until the brush just slightly touches into the paint. Gradually (one hair width between strokes) work out away from the color pile, moving back and forth until you see the blend you want on the blending path. What you see, is what you'll get on the project. This is why it is of utmost importance to keep a tidy palette. You will NEVER get a properly loaded brush from a messy, wider than the width of the brush you're using blending path.

Blend the color gradually to about 2/3's of the width of the bristles with the far side having just clean water. Color should not be worked more than about 3/4's of the way up the length of the bristles. Check yourself to be sure that the brush is resting square and flat against the palette as you stroke to load. If the brush handle is at too perpendicular an angle your color will not be able to flow evenly and gradually stop where it should. If there is a **strong narrow band of color that ends abruptly**, you have probably not stroked on the palette enough times, or perhaps your pressure against the palette is a bit too light. Don't press too hard or blend color only on the bristle tips. Firm pressure is needed to make the paint move gradually across the bristle width! If **COLOR FLOWS COMPLETELY ACROSS THE BRUSH WIDTH,** the blending path could be too wide, you could be angle stroking or the brush handle could be too perpendicular. The handle should be at about a 45 degree angle. You could also be stroking with too much space between each stroke. It may take a bit of time to get used to a different method of loading, but once you can stop thinking about every move you make, it will greatly **speed up your work**!! Blending on a wet palette lets you maintain maximum moisture and color in the brush during loading making the color go a great deal further as you paint, requiring less frequent loading! Also try to pull toward your body when painting as this is most comfortable and allows greater control over where the color goes. I constantly turn the work to allow a more comfortable counter-clockwise 11-7 angle. If your strokes feel either awkward or uncomfortable, change the position of your project to control your brush more comfortably and easily.

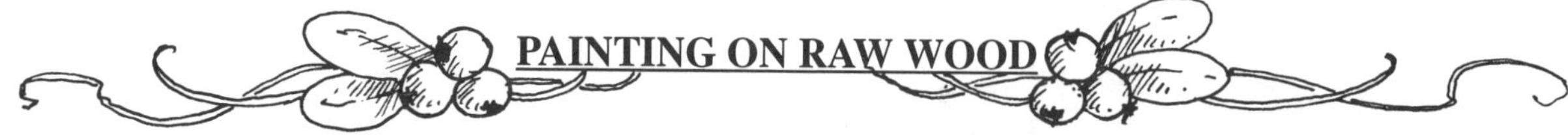

## PAINTING ON RAW WOOD

Although some do, **I ALMOST NEVER SEAL RAW WOOD** before painting! I **want** the paint to soak softly **into** the wood. It's my personal opinion, that the necessity of sealing wood is a carry-over from our oil painting days. If sealed, the paint won't seep into the wood grain as softly, smoothly or easily as with unsealed wood and the acrylic seals as you paint. The soft finished effect and raw wood allows me to easily achieve this softness. Be sure that the entire project piece is well sanded and tacked. Trace on the design with WHITE GRAPHITE. It may be a little hard to see on some pieces, but once you wet the area the white lines show up much more clearly. Well worn black graphite could also be used, but be very careful with new black graphite as the lines are very hard to cover with the sheer paint coverage I use. Begin work on the most forward area of the design. Lightly wet just the area you plan to paint with clean water. You will want to diminish the amount of water out toward the edge of the area to minimize bleeding into the next area. Use slightly more water in the brush if painting on raw wood. Sideload for floated color into acrylic color using the largest brush you comfortably can for the size of the area. This varies depending on experience. Color will appear slightly duller on a raw wood surface, giving it a soft antique effect. Float color as you normally would. **ALLOW EACH AREA TO DRY COMPLETELY**, before adding another layer of color! Since the colors have a tendency to "soak in" be sure to check again after the color is dry to be sure the values are as strong as you want them to be. Additional thin washes of the same color will intensify overall color after the floated color is in place. Keep forward areas more sheer and light and you then need to add only the strongest hard shines.

## STAINING YOUR PROJECTS

I often stain the entire piece, then add acrylic in just portions of the project. Add acrylic color on peg ends, portions of turned spindles or turned legs to accent them. I use MINWAX brand stains. Use any brand or hue you are comfortable with, but probably NOT a varnish/stain as it will probably be too slick. Wood should be well sanded and tacked clean before staining. Dry any stain a minimum of 8-12 hours before applying acrylic color to avoid chemical reaction between products.

## ACRYLIC BACKGROUNDS & COLOR BORDER DETAILING

**PETIFOUR SPONGES** are an indispensible painting tool! I apply all my acrylic background color with them. They are also wonderful for adding little accent borders on various projects! Use 2-3 coats of color for a totally opaque coverage. I find the Americana colors I use cover often with only one or two coats of color. Sand lightly just before the last coat of color with fine sand paper and tack off acrylic dust. You'll find petifours demonstrated on my video tapes. When using a round or oval as a template, float the outside shape including anything that extends beyond, then fill in the entire center with acrylic using a P-4. If a show of wood grain is desired, moisten the wood lightly, then use just a tiny bit of water with your acrylic color to **PICKLE** the surface. Allow to dry, adding another light wash if needed. Sand again with a brown grocery bag or a very fine sanding block.

To add a border of acrylic, I grasp the petifour securely between my thumb and middle finger. Work a small amount of color along one side of the sponge, allowing the paint to gradually flow part way across. Don't have too much color on the sponge, or it will leave a bead along the inner edge of your border. Adjust the width of the border by using the top of your thumb nail against the side of the piece to be bordered. Your index finger is used to keep the sponge firmly on the project surface and the middle finger keeps the finger & thumb firmly on the surface. Border two opposing sides and allow to dry, then do the two remaining sides. This gives a neat little square in each corner where the two layers overlap. Inner edges of borders can be left plain or decorated as desired. Practice on a wood scrap before going directly onto a project. It's really quick and easy once you get the swing of it!

## PAINTING TIDBITS

**FINISHING of the BACK & EDGES** is important! I often completely paint my design, then apply a couple of light coats of waterbase varnish over the painted surface. Be very careful not to allow any varnish to dribble onto the side areas to be stained or the stain won't take. When the varnish is dry, stain edges and back. I dry the stain decorated side up on either nail points or one of **WINNI MILLER'S DRY-IT BOARDS**. These plastic boards are great, especially for small things! I've also made my own larger drying board by driving groups of nails through a long plywood board to dry my projects without marring the paint or stain. You may want to have both at hand as it lets you work all sides at the same time. **VARNISHING** is usually done using a waterbase of good quality. There are many brands on the market. I use **DecoArt Brush-On Sealers**. When I've done something that will be receiving a lot of hard use like furniture, I use a good quality water clean-up polyurethane varnish from the local hardware store. Use an **exterior varnish** (water clean-up if you can find one) if your project is to be hung out doors.

### TRACING of the DESIGNS

I use WHITE GRAPHITE whenever possible especially on light background colors. Sometimes the background color doesn't allow us to see the white line clearly enough for accurate painting. Tilt the work to allow the light to catch the tracing, or lightly wet the surface to see the line more clearly or as a last resort, try well worn black graphite. I use **BLACK GRAPHITE** on a dark surface for the least amount of contrast while still being able to see the lines. Layers of floated color are quite sheer and you don't want lines showing through the finished painting. Test ANY graphite product to be sure that it is easily removed if necessary!!!

**Trace your design accurately ! Trace only the main design lines!** The detail lines in the drawing are done to give you a bit of perspective. They are placed in areas where the deepest shading values would occur. Use them as a reference only. Careless tracing can cause serious errors since most of us tend to follow whatever lines we trace. Sometimes only a slight line variance can destroy perspective and distort the design. Photocopy patterns using a heavy, good quality transparent paper such as Canson #110 Vidalon Vellum. I also use the Vellum if I want to accurately reduce or enlarge a design to fit a particular painting surface. Notice that I've done several designs several times or sizes on an alternative surfaces to help spur your imagination! If there are areas on your piece that need a filler, try adding a bit of holly and/or some strokework.

**CHALK PENCILS** are great for picking up missed portions or reinforcing pattern lines when necessary, as well as for making lines around templates. Be sure that they are of the type that can be easily removed with water.

A **PEEL-OFF MAGIC RUB STICK ERASER** #1960 lightly moistened with saliva will erase dry acrylic to the wood. Be careful.

**NOTE: To see details in photos more clearly, use a good magnifying glass!!!** You'll be absolutely amazed at the detail you will be able to see by magnifying the smaller areas of a color photo. This is especially helpful for those of us with older eyes!

**"Painter's Pal" STA-WET PALETTE!** It's hard to imagine being without it, and I'm always amazed to find that some of you have them and DON'T USE THEM! Maybe you just need a little shove! Soak the paper in a cylinder large enough to have the whole paper under water, at lease four hours before using. I've had paper soaking for weeks without damage to it. I use a spaghetti keeper, putting in 2 papers at a time. When I take out my last paper, I replace it with 2 more sheets. Always use the rag content paper refills from the company making your palette! It's doesn't deteriorate in water and costs about the same as tracing paper. I've found it to be transparent enough to see a strong black line drawing through it. It feels almost like an acrylic background when painting on the dry palette paper and works well to demo or practice painting or strokework.

Have **PLENTY OF WATER IN THAT SPONGE**! No amount of spraying over the top will take the place of well soaked paper and a sponge with all the water it will hold without coming up over the paper! Lay the soaked paper onto the saturated sponge, then take a tissue or paper towel and wipe back and forth across the top of the paper to remove any excess water from paper surface before laying out your paint. **PUT THOSE CORNER PIECES IN PLACE**. If you've lost them, write the company and get more! To receive new corners send a SASE to Masterson Ent., Inc. P.O. Box10775 Glendale, AZ 85318 and explain your needs. These corners are important to hold the paper tightly against the sponge, keeping air from drying the paper out! If you can't find a **Painter's Pal Sta-Wet Palette** call or write as we always keep them in stock. (price information on page 32) If you need more help using the palette you have with my painting methods, send us a legal size S.A.S.E.

**Top & Bottom Shape**
**for the center area of the cover sled pg. 6-7**
Connect top to bottom with a total straight side length of 10 1/2 inches from top to bottom corner.

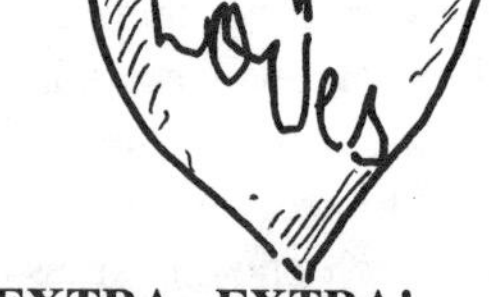


Santa

Snowmen

10 1/2" Total Length for SIDES

**EXTRA, EXTRA!**

Try using those **large nail files** and the **sanding blocks** used for smoothing applied fingernails for sanding your wood surfaces. If you have acrylic nails, ask your beautician for the cast-offs! Still lots of life left for us!!!

Use a **powdered blusher** for the cheeks on small faces, especially on fabric for a softer effect.

**FOR A LITTLE GLITZ** . . . Finish painting, then apply a layer of **Heavy Metal Clear Glimmer. Glamour Dust** over daubed on **Snow -Tex** while still wet is also a great snow in sunshine effect! All are from DecoArt.

**LOEW-CORNELL** makes brushes of an excellent quality! I use a series 7350 size 0 liner, 7300 series flat shaders, 7550 1/2" wash brush, 7520 filbert rakes in 1/4" and 1/2" and 7500 filberts. I'm especially grateful to have those **filbert rakes**! It sure speeds up painting all those Santa beards. Try using a Deerfoot stippler on your snowmen for a textured effect. Select Stipplers that don't have too long a bristle. Series #410 Deer Foot or the DM Stipplers are good. You can get a similar effect by using a flat shader side-loaded for floated color, the apply paint using a stippling motion. This is especially good when shading various areas of the snowmen.

**Fine Gold Edges** are really fast and easy if you use a **large nib Permanent Gold Markers**. Just pull the nib against a corner or sharp edge for a fast, straight gold border. Great on porcelain, thin wood, or routed edges on larger wood pieces, tin etc. Tape pennies on the bottom of a clear ruler to raise it enough to use the markers for straight lines without gold running under the ruler. There are a number of brands available, but it MUST have about a 1/8" wide nib so it will ride along a sharp edge. Watch new pens. The ink can run out pretty fast at first. Test the ink on a scrap of wood to be sure it really IS permanent! If it smears when you apply waterbase varnish over it, be sure to spray it with a matte spray before using your regular brush-on varnishes.

I know you will find lots more ways to use a little extra gold once you have a pen of your own!

Use DecoArt **Glorious Gold** for a duller gold and **Emperor's Gold** for brighter gold strokework or edging.

## ACRYLIC TO OIL CONVERSION

It has been years since I've worked in oils, but perhaps this will be of some help to you. It also converts from Americana to Folk Art.

| DecoArt Americana Brand | Folk Art Brand | POSSIBLE COMPARABLE OIL COLOR |
|---|---|---|
| BUTTERMILK | Tapioca | Rembrandt Naples Yellow Light Extra |
| SNOW WHITE | Wicker White | Titanium White |
| EBONY | Licorice | Ivory Black |
| MIDNITE GREEN | Wrought Iron | Payne's Gray |
| CHARCOAL GREY | W.Iron + Coffee Bean | |
| OLIVE GREEN | | Rembrandt Cinnebar Green Light |
| LT. AVOCADO | Green Olive | Yellow Ochre + Sap Green (2-1) or your favorite leaf mix |
| PLANTATION PINE | Southern Pine | Rembrandt Greenish Umber |
| GOLDEN STRAW | Buttercup | Naples Yellow |
| HONEY BROWN | English Mustard | Yellow Ochre |
| YELLOW OCHRE | Camel | Raw Sienna + Naples Yellow Light Extra (2-1) |
| RAW SIENNA | Honeycomb | Raw Sienna |
| MILK CHOCOLATE | Nutmeg | Burnt Umber |
| DARK CHOCOLATE | Coffee Bean | Grumbacher Raw Umber or any grey/brown umber |
| DRIFTWOOD | Platinum Grey | Rembrandt Warm Gray + Titanium White (3-1) |
| NEUTRAL GRAY | Dapple Grey | Rembrandt Warm Gray |
| BLUE MIST | Teal Blue | Cerulean Blue + Titanium White (1-5) |
| BLUE GRAY DUST | | Shiva Ice Blue |
| DEEP MIDNITE BLUE | Indigo | Prussian Blue + just a touch of Paynes Gray |
| BRANDY WINE | Paprika | Rembrandt Red Iron Oxide or Cad. Red Light + Burnt Sienna (3-1) |
| (Red Iron Oxide*) | Rusty Nail | Cadmium Red Light, blend Cad. Yellow Med. in the forward areas |
| TRUE RED | | Grumbacher Red |
| NAPA RED | | |
| CRANBERRY WINE | Mendocino (Ceramcoat) | Alizeran Crimson |
| RUSSET | Huckleberry | Rembrandt Burnt Carmine |
| **SKIN COLORS** | | **Use Rembrandt's "BARRICK FLESH SET"** |
| Hilite White | white | |
| Fleshtone | Skintone | |
| Medium Flesh | Chocolate Parfait | |
| Shading Flesh | Brown Sugar | |
| Brandy Wine (blush) | Paprika | |

Color is truly in the eye of the beholder. Don't become "hung up" on what I use. For example, if I've painted something medium blue, and you have a combination of colors in at least three values of blue that pleases **YOUR EYE**, go ahead and use it if you don't have exactly what I've used or until you can purchase my combination if you choose to do so! Just relax, have fun, and go with what **you** like!!!

## *SEMINARS or VIDEOS With Jean Zawicki*

I've had numerous requests to make a video of my techniques available. We now offer four 2-Hr. **Home Videos** to help understand my painting methods. I've developed an expedient method of painting with acrylics and I do my best to show you exactly how I work. Each video has information on supplies, brush loading, floating color, miscellaneous things like gold leaf or strokework and a project complete with photographs and written instructions for the projects demonstrated. Tape #1 has gold leafing and a basic Santa Face, Tape #2 has strokework and a larger more detailed Santa face, #3 is a **floral group** with roses, daisies, forget-me-nots, leaves etc. and #4 is a **fruit group** including raspberries, plums, holly, blueberries and more.

**Send a legal size SASE for an information sheet describing the different selections or call using Visa or Mastercard.**

To fully understand another persons painting techniques, nothing beats hands-on experience! The videos are an excellent follow-up to review seminar materials. To me, the most important thing is to make you "really see the world around you" with the project helping to illustrate what we need to understand about the subject we're painting. Each year I schedule a very limited number of seminars around the country. In 1994 we opened White Horse Bed & Breakfast and we're really enjoying our guests now that the hard work of getting the house "guest friendly" is finished. Because we're in a tourist area, I am unable to travel teach during June, July and August. I have a booth at the National convention, so am busy preparing for that in April and May and can't travel. I try to schedule my travel teaching during the remaining months. Since it is so limited, I find I really look forward to being with other painters more than ever. Teaching is something I really miss! I sincerely hope we can someday paint together. Failing that, I've tried to put as much as I possibly could into each of my 2-Hr. home videos for those wanting more understanding of my painting methods. It's the next best thing to being there - and we'll still be painting together!!!

# SANTA LOVES SNOWMEN

Here is the cover project & book title I woke with at Mary Riley's in Mossy Head, Florida between the Jacksonville and Pensacola Chapter seminars. It was the sign I had awaited before deciding to do "one more" book!

The sled is dear to my heart for yet another reason. In 1995, Louise Mangham attended a seminar in WI. She, Bob and I became immediate friends. This sled will be presented to DAC at the 1997 Nat'l. Convention by the So. Bay Folk Artists in Louise's memory. She loved my Santa's, and her painting friends in California chose this piece as a tribute to this very special lady.
May we all paint with Louise again someday at a seminar in the sky.

**The graceful sled I used for the cover design is from Wayne's Woodenware.**

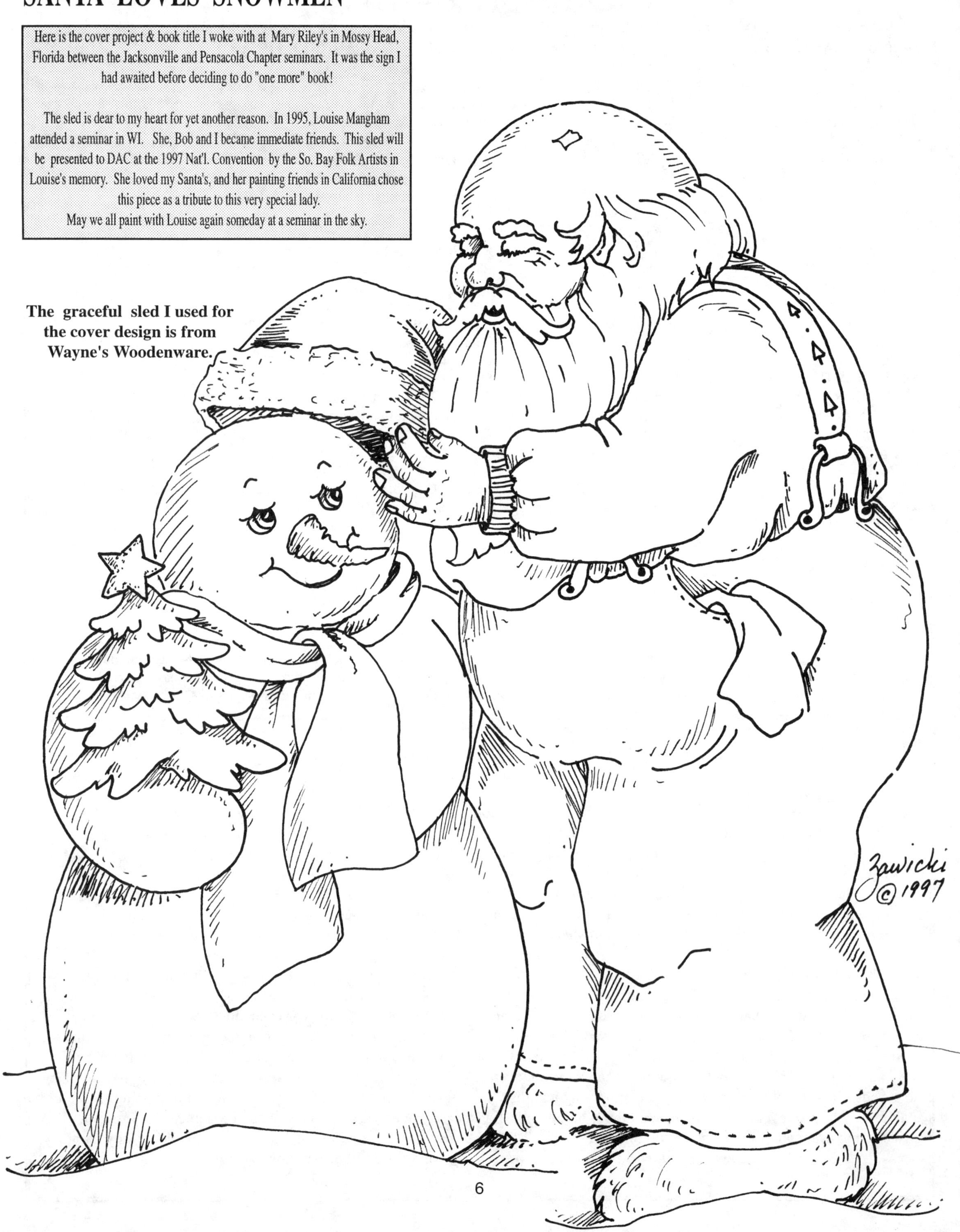

**SLED PREPARATION:** You can use any shape you like to create a painting vignette. Ovals, circles or any shape, as long as the majority of the design fits within the shape. Put the entire shape on tracing paper and fold it in half, doing 1/2 of any curves, then flipping it over to trace the second half. I've given you the top and bottom curved shapes I came up with for my sled. I measured 1" in from either side for the straight sides. You can often get the center round and oval mat cut-outs from your local frame shop as they usually throw them away. They make wonderful vignette templates! Papier mache' boxes, dishes etc. are also sometimes good shapes for vignettes. Just find something that is approximately the right size and go for it. I floated a little **Milk Chocolate + Dark Chocolate** around the outside of the vignette, then added some **Deep Midnite Blue** strokework with a liner.

I like to have at least one small portion of the design extending out into background stain if possible. Note that only a tiny bit of Santa's boops and a little of the bottom part of the snowman extend beyond the side lines. I will fade the snow lines out into background also, but that doesn't require any preliminary plan. Trace on the shape of the entire vignette on tracing paper, then position the pattern to see where any portion will extend outside the vignette. Trace just that small area, and background it with the rest of the vignette. I've done my background with **Blue Grey Mist**. Float in the outside edge of the vignette's shape with a 1" wash brush, then fill in the center area with the same brush using a criss-cross "X" strokes. The lights and shadows that naturally occur with this method create a soft atmospheric background effect. You can add DMB or white as desired while doing the background to create even more value variation. Allow to dry, then add more color if too much grain is still showing. Trace on the main design with white graphite, matching up areas that extend beyond the vignette.

**PAINTING THE DESIGN:** Undercoat Santa's face, hand, hankie, the suspender (not the end fasteners), the star on the tree and the snowman's scarf with **Buttermilk**. Follow directions for painting Santas & Snowmen on page 14 & 19 for painting snowmen, Santa faces and beards. For this background, I was able to let the background do most of the color for the beard. I just added streaks of soft **Charcoal Grey** to establish the flow of the hair. The white with the Filbert Rake does the rest.

**THE TREE, STAR, SCARF, HANKIE & SUSPENDER:** Float in the shape of each of the branch tips with **Lt. Avocado**. Shade up under the overhanging branch with **Plantation Pine**. Highlight with just a hint of **Jade Green** or if a warmer effect is desired, use **Olive Green**. Use the greens for the Wintergreen runner design, adding red berries and long pine needles on the raggedy **Charcoal Grey** branches. The star is washed with **Yellow Ochre** then shaded with **Raw Sienna**. Snow could be added If you wish. Add the tiny little triangular tree shapes of the suspenders with the tree greens. Shade the hanky shape with the **Midnite Green** and add **Lt. Avocado** stripes with a #2 flat. Add fine lines of **Brandy Wine** in the opposite direction if you want a plaid hanky. Shade the trees with **Plantation Pine** and add a small trunk line of **Charcoal Grey.** Highlight with **Jade Green**. Shade with **Russet**. Add some small dip-dots of Brandy Wine on the suspenders.

**SANTA'S PANTS & FUR SHOES:** I floated the pants shape with **Deep Midnite Blue**. I like a slightly duller deep blue, so I add a bit of **Midnite Green** in the whole bottle to dull and darken the color. The background color becomes the light value for the blue pants. I applied the **Deep Midnite Blue** on the edges of the sled with a petifour sponge. For Santa's fur shoes, I loaded a #8 flat shader for floating color, then slid the brush along on the chisel edge to create the long fluffy fur effect with **Charcoal Grey**.

**SANTA'S SHIRT & HAT:** Float in the shape of the hat and shirt with **Warm Neutral Toning** to neutralize the background color. Add washes of the same color until you no longer see the blue background reflecting through. Shape and shade in the hat and shirt with **Brandy Wine**. Allow the WNT to create light forward values. Add deep shadows with **Russet**. As an option, adding some very fine lines of **Russet** on the shirt to make it appear to be a knit garment. Use **Yellow Ochre, Raw Sienna & Dark Chocolate** stippled in to create the lamb's wool fur hat trim and also for the leather straps that attach the suspenders.

Using a large flat shader, lightly float a hint of **Midnite Green** above the snow lines. Float **Snow White** with a #10 flat or 1/2" wash brush beneath the lines to create the snow drifts, fading the light value blending down until in melts into the background color. Pull color out slightly beyond the vignette borders. I used **Silver Sage Green + White** for a hint of background lighting around the figure.

***SIDE RUNNER DESIGN***

*Words & top and bottom shapes are on Page 4*

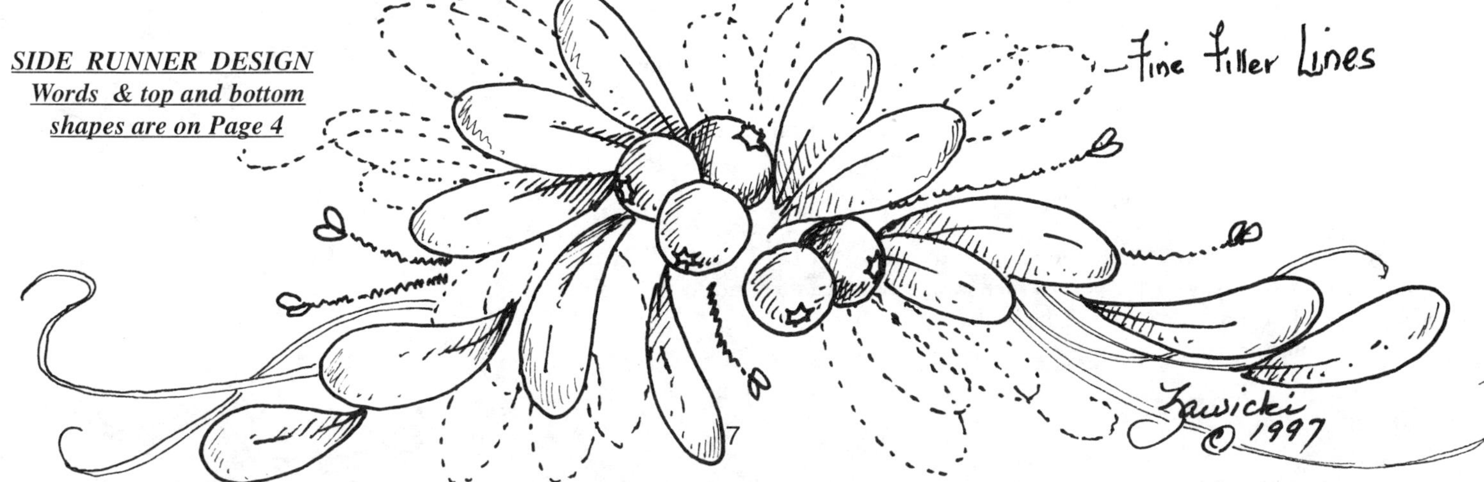

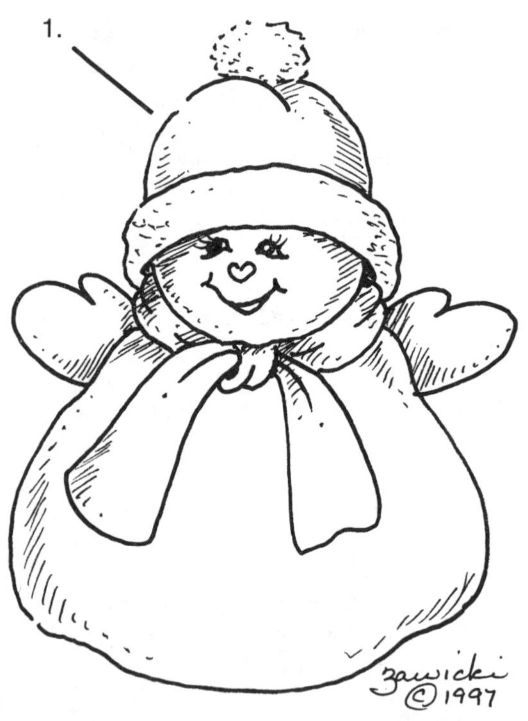


# Snow Folks Don't Have All The Fun!

*These little fellows are extremely versatile! Whether you plant them among greenery and dried materials in a cheese box lid, or drill holes in their arms to add wire to create door hangers, they'll bring a smile every time they peek out from their special spot. Given a bit of time, you'll find lots of ways to use them. They're fast and easy to do, and can be good to use as ornaments in the reduced sizes given, or go to a copy machine and enlarge to your hearts desire! Follow the general directions for painting the snowmen's body areas on page 19. I'll give you colors for the details on each of the pieces.*

## ***SAMMY SNOW-BOY:***

*(Left)* I've painted an ornament cut-out and done one of a neat little heart puzzle adding some snowballs on a **Warm Neutral Toning** background. An enlarged version for a 1/2" pine cut-out is used on the pine wreath & also on a round box.

**FOR THE WREATH:**

Float the hat top in with **Buttermilk**, adding **Santa Red** stripes with a fine liner. The mittens, hat band and tassel are all **lt. Avocado** shaded with **Plantation Pine**. The scarf is floated in with **Jade Green** and shaded with Plantation Pine. Use **Santa Red** for the stripes.

For the 10" wreath I added **Snow-Tex** to small pine cones and dried fruit slices with a palette knife, then sprinkled on **Glamour Dust**. Allow to dry, then hot glue them into the wreath. I cut apart icicle garland and glued in individual icicles too. Tiny birds were glued onto both these cut-outs. Paint in birds if creating a scene on flat surfaces.

To use a 1/2" pine cut-out for door knob hangers, drill a small hole in each hand and attach 18 gauge wire to create a hanger. You can either leave the wire hanger smooth, attach some small red hearts and or wind part of the hanger around a pencil to make little loops for a more decorative touch. A second version is on a beautiful 6" round box from **Wood 'n Things** with a **Russet** background.

## ***CHILLY CHARLIE***

*Charlie gets cold ears, so he wears a warm woolen cap with ear flaps to chase away the chill! He also is a good boy and always wears his boots like all northern snow-kids do.*

**(Below)** Done in the size given for an ornament, Charlie was then enlarged and cut from 1/2" pine & used on an 8" cheese box lid.

**ON THE LID:** The hat is floated in with **Raw Sienna** then shaded with **Milk Chocolate**. Use the **Santa Red** shading with **Cranberry Wine** for the hat band. Highlight with **Buttermilk**.

Use **Lt. Avocado** shading with **Plantation Pine** for the scarf and one of the patches. The other patch is done with **Russet** and the fringe is **Santa Red**. I used **Charcoal Gray** and a fine liner for the stitches around the patches. Float in the heart with **Santa Red** and shade it with **Russet**. The boots are floated in with **Charcoal Gray**. Shade with a bit of **Midnite Green** - highlight with white.

The 8" cheese box lid is one I've had around for a long time. Adjust the enlargement to the size lid or wreath you have, hot gluing 1" pine garland around the outside edge of the lid. Glue various greenery and dried materials at either side after hot gluing Sammy at the center bottom inside of the box lid, then add one of those cute tiny little birds on his arm.

Shading on the bodies of all the snow-kids was done with just a hint of **Charcoal Gray**. Any of these snowmen would be great reduced to lapel pin size also!!! For ornaments I paint the backs as shown in the center color pages, but not for pins or wreaths.

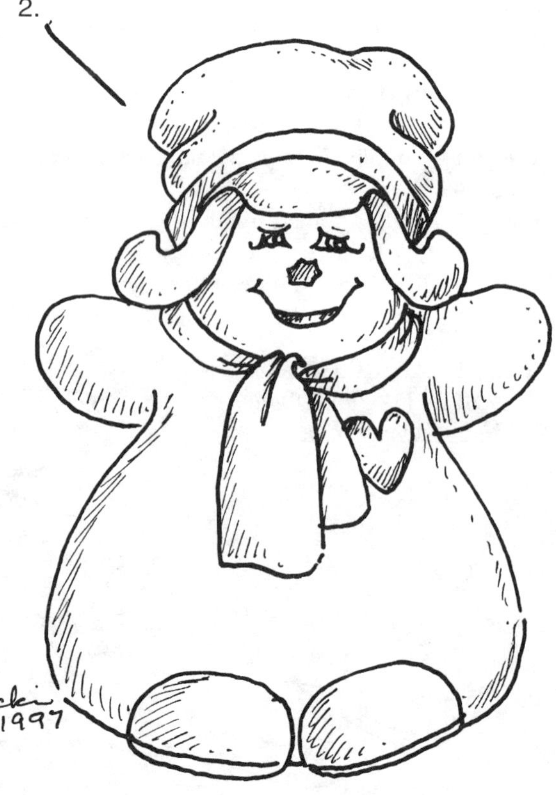

***DAPPER DUDLEY:*** *Change Dudley's or any of the snow folks colors to suit your own taste, adding a bit of strokework by referring to page 27. Add little trimmings to create a variety of effects. I enlarged Dudley to fit the little box from Wayne's Woodenware, then stained the box Puritan Pine. Shade around the figure with **Charcoal Grey.***

**THE BOX:** With a liner, make a little wiggley-line/dot border in **Plantation Pine**. Dry, then lightly stain out from the border & edges with **Lt. Avocado**. I added a bit of **Glamour Dust** over the white snow while the acrylic was wet. Float in the hat and vest with **Desert Sand**. Shade them first with **Raw Sienna** then **Charcoal Grey.** His broom handle is Charcoal and the bottom is **Yellow Ochre** shaded with **Raw Sienna & Milk Chocolate**. The bow tie and one patch are **Lt. Avocado** as is the trim on the vest. Use **Brandy Wine** for the heart patch shading with **Cranberry Wine**. See him also as an ornament cut-out.

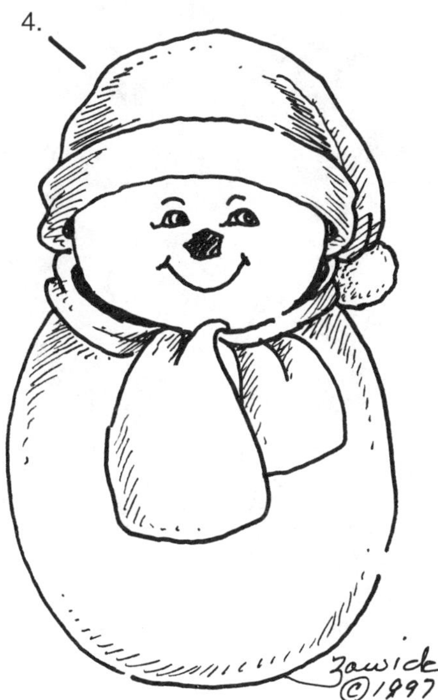


## FLAKY FRED

*Any of the smaller designs can be enlarged to fit these great little door knob hangers from Zim's. Enlarge Freddie to fit.*

For a trick that really "fools the eye", allow the background color to do as much work as you can with the painting. On the door hanger from **Zim"s**, I painted the surface with **Blue Mist**. Trace with white graphite, minus stripes for the little snowman at left. No short-cuts for painting the snowman, but I shaded the entire hat and scarf with just a hint of **Blue Haze + Midnite Green** brush-blended. Now, pick up **Medium Flesh** full across a #2 flat shader and draw the color across an area to create a stripe. Shade the stripes with a little **Shading Flesh**. Highlight down the middle of both pieces with a touch of **Hi-lite Flesh**. Use these colors for lettering and border too.

You'll also find Freddie done on Warm Neutral Toning background using the same "fool the eye" minimal painting on one of the little heart puzzles. I used **Dusty Rose, Mauve, & Brandy Wine** for the hat and scarf on the puzzle. Also do him as a little ornament using any of your favorite colors.

**THE FROSTY FRIENDS NAPKIN HOLDER (below)** *The napkin holder came from Wayne's too. The wood was stained Puritan Pine, then I painted the half oval area of the front with **Warm Neutral Toning.** As with the blue background above, I allowed the background to be the main clothing color as well as the background, as much as I could. I also painted them on watercolor paper and inserted them in one of the neat 2-pc. lucite pencil holders from **Herr's Inc,** using **Brandy Wine** shaded with **Cranberry Wine** for the clothing . Use the colors below for the napkin holder.*

**TOP HAT: Charcoal Grey**
**SCARF:** Float in the shape with **Med. Flesh**, add stripes with a #2 flat and **Shading Flesh**. Touch lightly into **Russet** for shadows.
**HAT BAND & STOCKING CAP TOP: Shading Flesh.** Brighten with a bit of **Brandy Wine.**
**FUR TRIM: Milk Chocolate** shaded with **Dark Chocolate.**
**BACKGROUND SHADING: Russet + Charcoal Grey**.

Use a fairly large flat shader and very wet, small amounts of color. Blot on your wet paper towel if you think you have too much color. Draw a small border using a fine liner and trim the edges of the napkin holder with **Russet**.

Everyone has different color preferences. This is an easy project to allow you to use your own personal favorites! Try them as an ornament or lapel pin cut-out too!

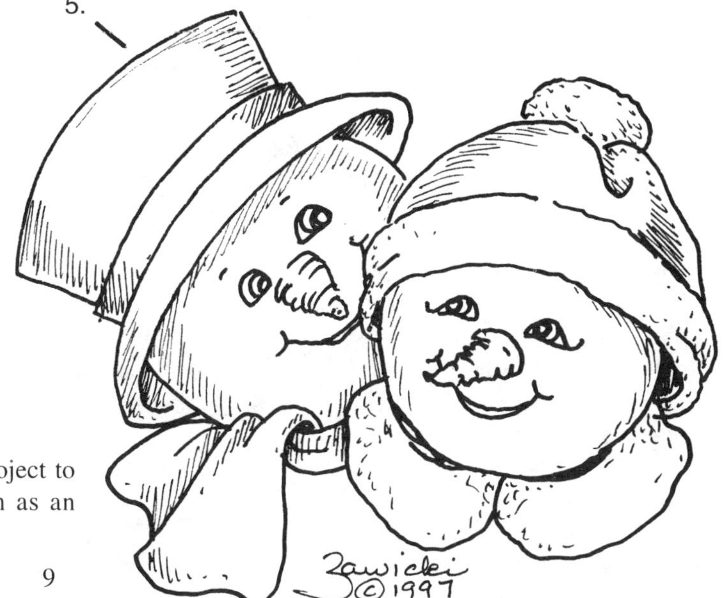

# Mrs. Snowtapple's Sweet Tweets

*Use this adorable heart plate from Wayne's Woodenware with or without the glass liner. The verse on the rim relays your good wishes, and imagine the guests delight when the cookies are gone and Mrs. Snowtapple and friends smile up at them!*

**WOOD PREPARATION:**

I use a fairly solid wash of **Evergreen** on the rim and back of the plate. Slightly moisten the surface, then apply very slightly thinned color with a pre-moistened petifour sponge. Using a Winnie Noah **Dry-It Board** will allow you to work on both sides without waiting for the first side to dry. I used a fairly solid color coverage, but still allowed a bit of the wood grain to show through the color, especially on the back. Lazy lady doesn't want to do 2-3 coats if she can avoid it!

When the green is dry, apply **Cranberry Wine** on the thickness edge of the plate and on the round routed bead between the rim and center of the plate. I used the petifour for the edge, but switched to a brush to keep the bordering rounded bead more tidy. Allow to dry, then with a petifour sponge, apply two coats of **Silver Sage Green** in the center of the plate.

Trace on the design with white graphite, and the lettering with dark graphite.

**PAINTING THE DESIGN**: Use snow man techniques for Mrs. Snowtapple's body. The little coals for her buttons, her eyes and the shading on the snow beneath her and shadows around the figure were done with **Midnite Green**. The branch arms are done lightly using a #1 flat and some **Charcoal Grey**. Allow the background to be your light value.

**JACKET:** Float in the shape with **Lt. Avocado** then shade it with **Evergreen**.

**HAT:** Float in the shape with **Cranberry Wine** and shade with a bit of **Black Plum**. Use the jacket colors for the hat band, even though a good bit will be covered when you add the snow on the hat brim.

**SCARF:** Float in the shape with **Yellow Ochre** and shade with a brush-blend of **Raw Sienna** with just enough **Evergreen** to grey the color a bit. Add **Cranberry Wine** stripes with a fine liner to both the scarf and jacket.

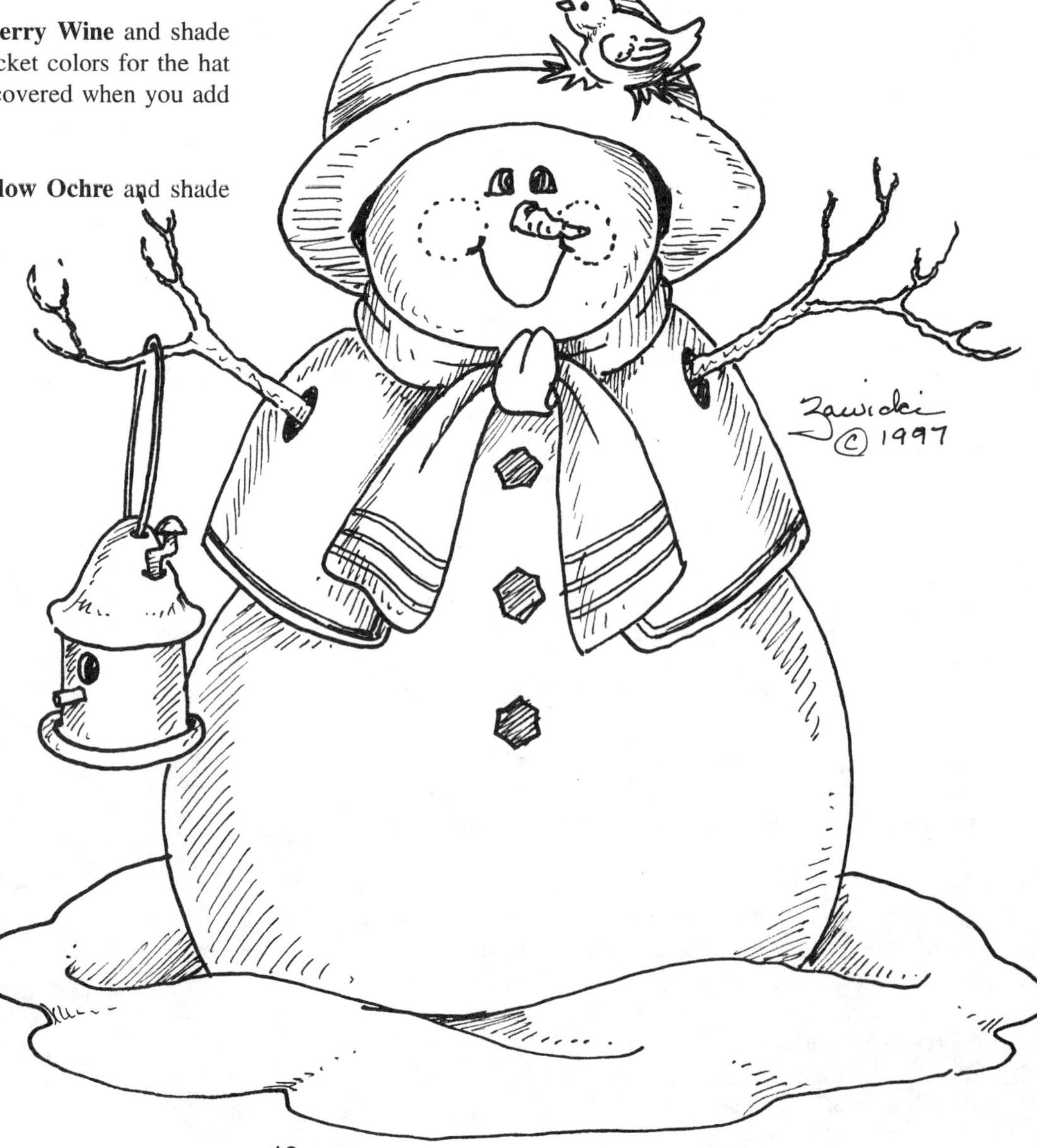


**BIRDHOUSE & BIRD:** Use **Blue Mist** to float in the shape of the body of the bird house and the bird. Shade them with **Williamsburg Blue**. Draw in the little ribbon on the branch with a liner and the same blues. The roof and bottom of the birdhouse are floated in with **Yellow Ochre** and shaded with **Raw Sienna.** The perch, line around the hole and chimney roof are **Cranberry Wine**. Use the **Yellow Ochre** for the straw nest of the bird, but shade that with **Honey Brown**. The hanging string and chimney are done with **Charcoal Grey**.

Snowflakes are added with a liner and white. First do a large cross, then a smaller "x", then a dip-dot of white at the center where they intersect. Use **Sno-Tex** for the textured snow areas, adding Glimmer if you wish.

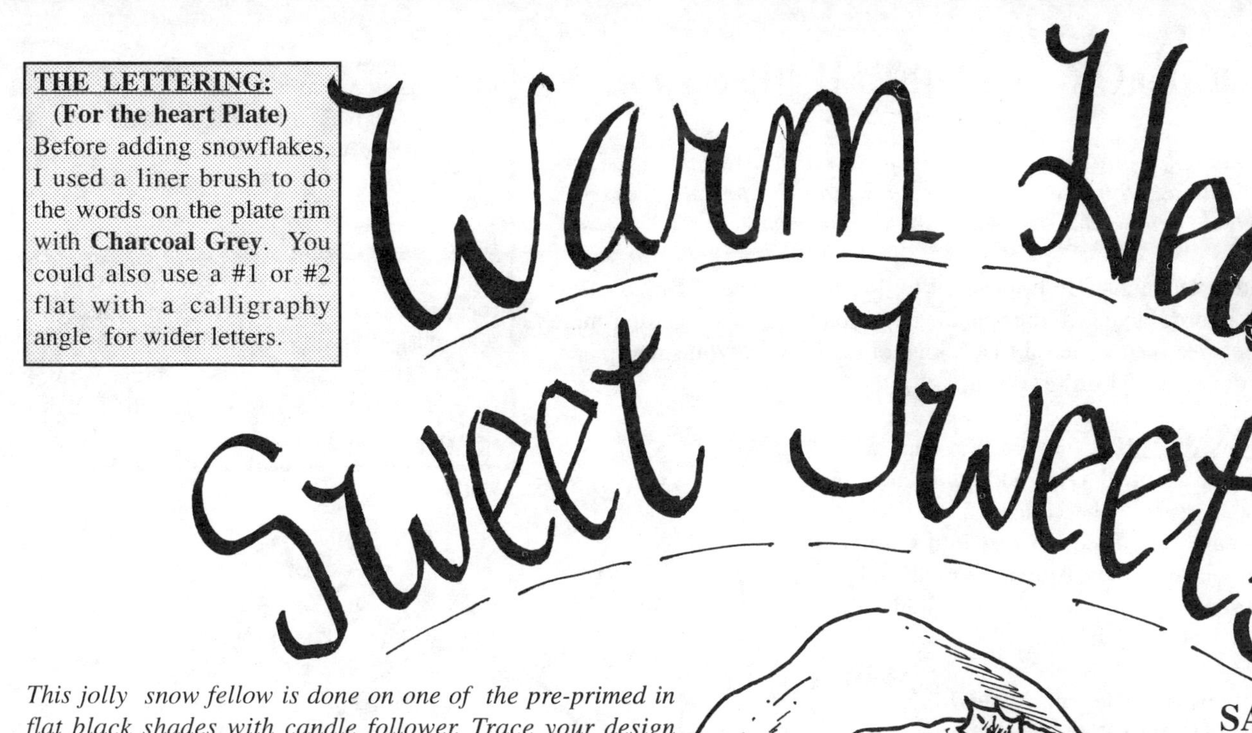


**THE LETTERING:**
**(For the heart Plate)**
Before adding snowflakes, I used a liner brush to do the words on the plate rim with **Charcoal Grey**. You could also use a #1 or #2 flat with a calligraphy angle for wider letters.

**SANTA'S HELPER!**
*Candle follower from* ***Viking Woodcrafts****.*

*This jolly snow fellow is done on one of the pre-primed in flat black shades with candle follower. Trace your design with black graphite. They also have the square shouldered straight candles to use with the followers.*

Before you begin to paint on a non-porous surface, remember that you MUST allow at least 15-30 minutes drying time between layers of color! If you don't, you can experience unsightly lifting that is hard to repair. Also, keep your pressure feather light! I outlined the facial features with Buttermilk before adding any color. Paint over the hat berries, then trace or free-hand them in later on. The leaves are just little strokes, so do try to just undercoat your berry clusters, then free-hand the leaves with Lt. Avocado tipped into **Plantation Pine or Evergreen** using a #2 Filbert brush. Paint the berries as you normally would. I used the browns for the fur, adding a bit of background lighting with a hint of **Blue Grey Mist**. Undercoat the hat with first floated, then washes of **Warm Neutral Toning**. I then floated on **Brandy Wine** shading with **Cranberry Wine**. Gold is applied with a wide nib permanent gold pen. He would also make a great little ornament cut-out. Change the hat colors for more variety.

## ICICLE IKE:

*This one is done on one of the little 4 1/2 x 6" photo albums from* ***Dalee Book Co.*** *of Brooklyn, NY 11217. I backgrounded a 4x6" photo frame to match it. Dalee products are readily available at many shops.*

2.

**PREP:** The pieces were carefully backgrounded with **Medium Flesh** using a petifour sponge. Give the pieces two light coats of color. Dry thoroughly with each application, then use a natural rough sea sponge to lightly stipple on some **Warm Neutral Toning** then just a little **Buttermilk**. White veins can be added if desired. For the hat and scarf I floated in the shapes then washed until I lost most of the mottled background with **Shading Flesh**. Shade with **Brandy Wine** and highlight with **Hi-lite Flesh**. Add stripes with **Shading Flesh +** a touch of **Brandy Wine.** I painted the hat band and undercoated the bell with **Buttermilk.** Finish the bell with **Golden Straw & Raw Sienna**. Shade the hat band with **Charcoal + Midnite Green**. I lettered the words "SPECIAL MEMORIES" with **Charcoal Grey** on the front, then painted various sized snowflakes in remaining areas and on the frame with a liner and pure white acrylic. You could also paint the outside edge with a darker color if you would like to create a border effect.

Zawicki © 1997

# WINTER COLD FOR FEATHERED FRIENDS!

*Here in the north, feeding the birds is essential for their survival. We enjoy two large families of Cardinals along with many other birds all through our cold Wisconsin winter. This is for all my fellow bird care-givers all over the country!*

Use snowman painting techniques from page 19 to do the snowman figure. Allow the background color to do some of your shading for you if you can, adding more shadows to create perspective as needed. He's kind of a silly guy, with small pieces of coal for a mouth done with **Midnite Green**.

This was done on a wood piece I've had forever, but I liked the shape. You could use it on any wood piece you have handy. Sleds or welcome signs would be good.

Stain the entire piece **Puritan Pine** then apply 2-3 coats of **Deep Midnite Blue** on the painting surface. Trace the design with dark graphite. Splattered snow was added after painting was complete using thinned white acrylic on an old brush drawn across a palette knife.

**WEATHERED SIGN & PAIL:** Float in the shape with **Driftwood**. Shade with **Neutral Grey** adding a touch of **Charcoal Grey** if necessary. The corn in the bucket is done with a very small flat. I side-loaded into **Golden Straw** then caught a bit of **Honey Brown** along the edge and just daubed the color in at random. Highlight with **Taffy Cream**. Lettering is **Charcoal**.

**PINE TREE:** Float in the shape with **Avocado Lt.** shading it with **Plantation Pine** and adding a bit of light value with **Jade Green**. The snow on this one was lightly stippled in with a #10 flat and white after everything else was done.

**HAT & SCARF:** Float in the hat with **Raw Sienna**. Shade it with some **Milk Chocolate** and highlight it with **Yellow Ochre + Buttermilk**. The hat band is floated in with **Warm Neutral Toning** then shaded with **Brandy Wine.** Highlight with white. Use the same colors for the scarf, using the Brandy Wine for the stripes.

**BIRD:** Use **Williamsburg Blue** shading it with **Deep Midnite Blue** and highlighting it with a really pale blue like **Silver Sage Green**. Use yellow values for the beak and Midnite Green for the eyes.

**BIRDHOUSE:** Mainly **Brandy Wine** shaded with **Russet** and highlighted with **Hi-Lite Flesh** and **Charcoal Grey** for the base and long roof line. Add **Taffy Cream** teardrop shingles outlined with **Raw Sienna**.

**FINISHING:** If you have routing around the edges, protect the area with masking tape. Draw the bristles of a worn-out brush filled with thinned white acrylic across the edge of a palette knife blade to create snow. Keep it mostly on the dark blue evening sky background. Varnish.

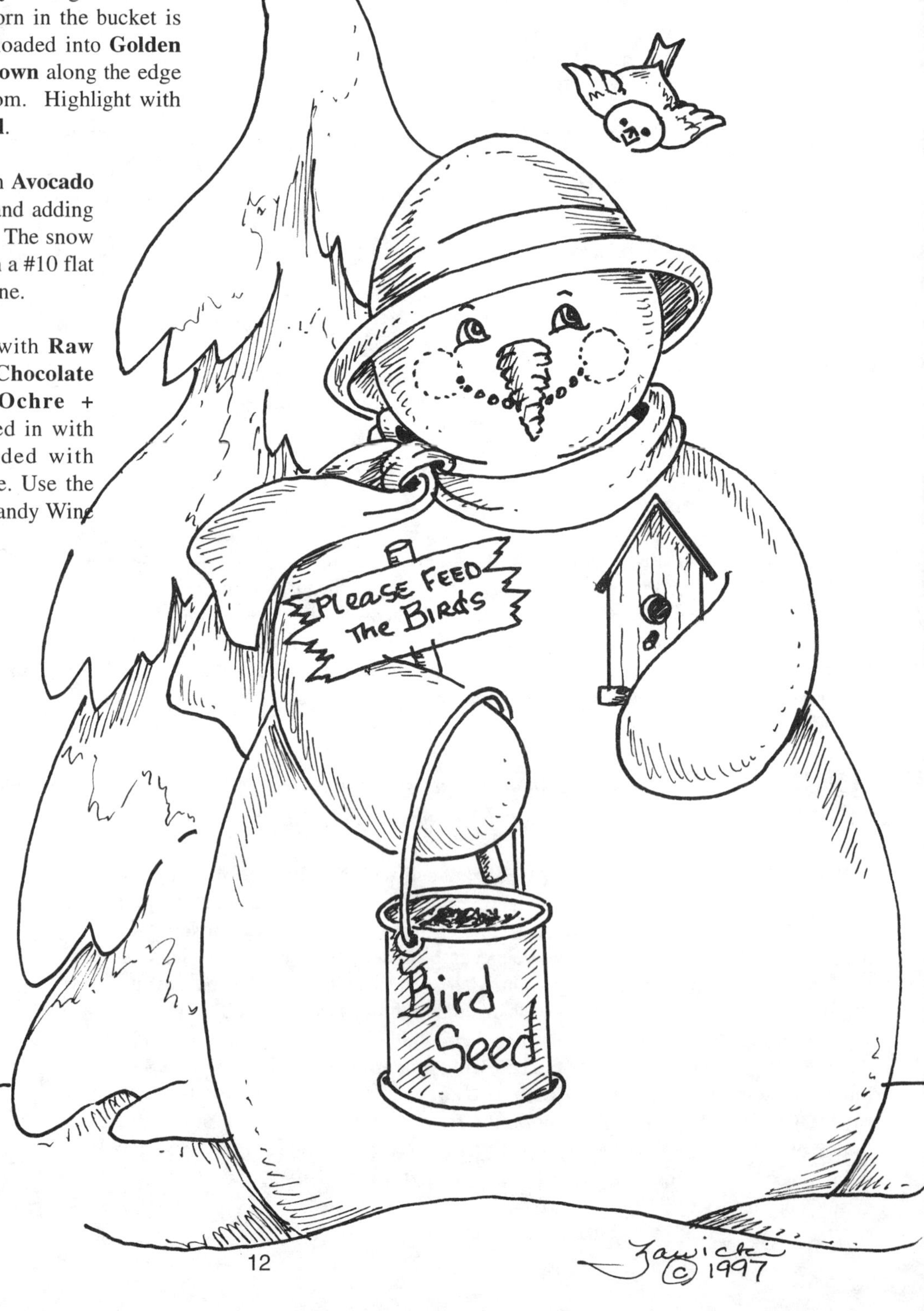

# LITTLE ROBIN RED BREAST WITH ST. NICK

***When I found this little angular heart in Florida I fell in love, so here's the shape!***

Paint the top surface **Warm Neutral Toning.** It's easy to free-hand in the intertwined branches and leaves, so trace on the berries and free-hand branches, adding stroke leaves with a #4 flat. Use the background for the main hat color, shading with **Mauve** and just a hint of **Brandy Wine. Use** Midnite Green for blossom ends. The berries are **Brandy Wine** shaded with **Napa Red**. The hat band is **Buttermilk** shaded with **Charcoal Grey**. Use **Golden Straw** shaded with **Honey Brown** for the sleigh bell. Highlight all with white.

The Robin is **Charcoal Grey** with a soft orange breast (**Yellow Ochre + Brandy Wine**) and some white to the rear of the body bottom. Use regular greens for the leaves, then pull in the branches using a #1 flat side-loaded into **Charcoal**. Highlight with a hint of **Buttermilk**. Shade around the figure with a light brush-blend of **Russet & Charcoal Grey**. The back and side edges are **Russet.** See basic instruction for the Santa Face.

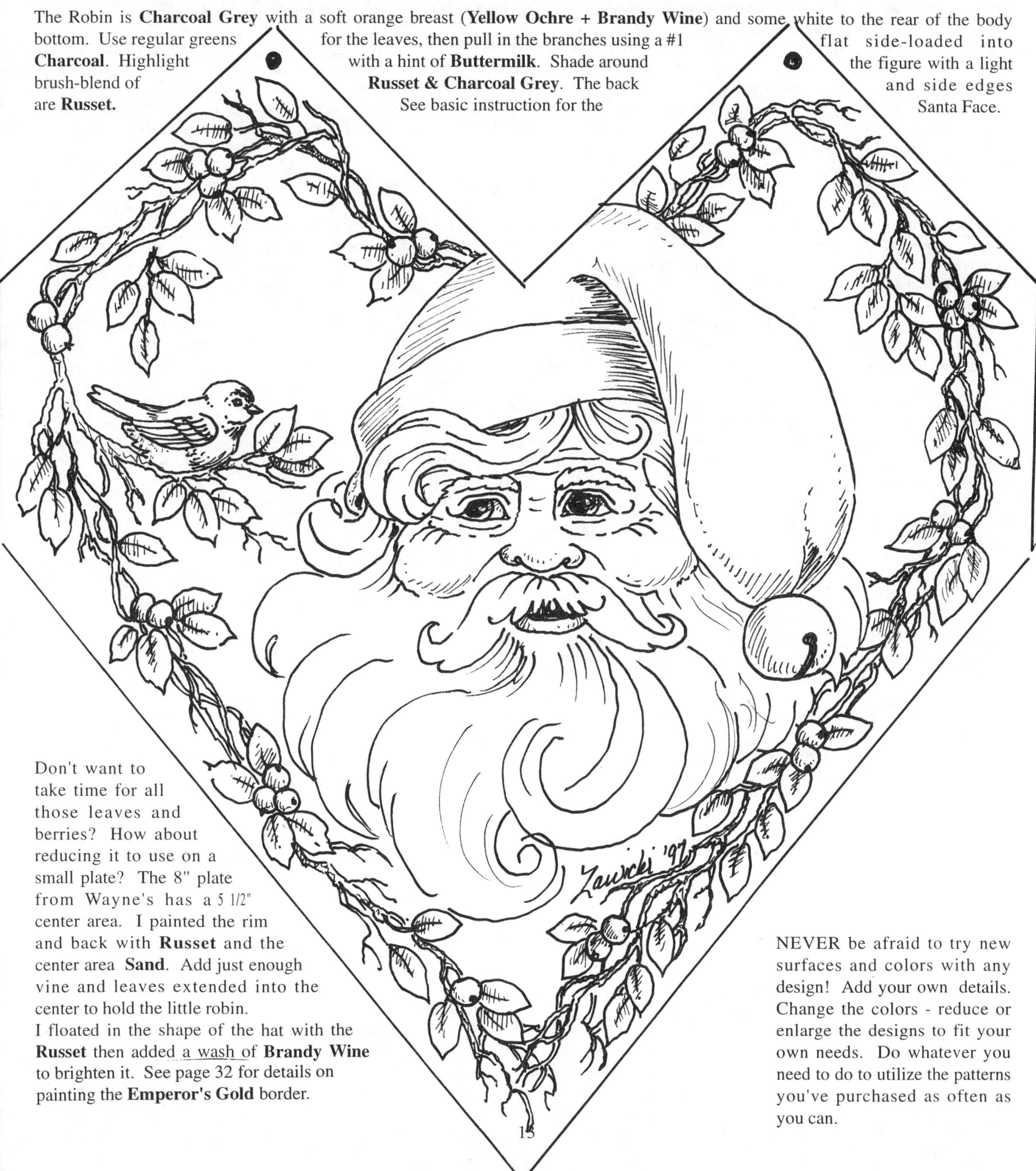


Don't want to take time for all those leaves and berries? How about reducing it to use on a small plate? The 8" plate from Wayne's has a 5 1/2" center area. I painted the rim and back with **Russet** and the center area **Sand**. Add just enough vine and leaves extended into the center to hold the little robin.

I floated in the shape of the hat with the **Russet** then added a wash of **Brandy Wine** to brighten it. See page 32 for details on painting the **Emperor's Gold** border.

NEVER be afraid to try new surfaces and colors with any design! Add your own details. Change the colors - reduce or enlarge the designs to fit your own needs. Do whatever you need to do to utilize the patterns you've purchased as often as you can.

**PAINTING REALISTIC SANTA FACES - with Zawicki**

**ILL. 1 UNDERCOATING THE FACE:** Always float in the face shape with a soft white such as **Buttermilk** when they are on either dark backgrounds, or on lighter values of blues and greens, adding washes until the background darkness is neutralized. Light Pink backgrounds such as **Warm Neutral Toning** can replace the lightest skin value. Darker pinks will dull the brightness of the face, so undercoat them also. TRACE CAREFULLY, then use floated color for all but the washes. This is one of your most important steps in face painting, so proceed carefully! Balance and shape each of the features, going **AROUND** the outside of the line shaping **the eyes** and **ON** the inside of the line for **the nose** tip. Notice that the nose width consist of three separate parts. The two side nostrils should total about 1/4 of the width each, and the bulbous end uses the remaining half. With a broad smile, the width of the nose broadens as the nostrils flare. This goes along with upturned mouths and eyes for a "happier" look! Check at this time to be sure that your eyes are similarly shaped & sized. Create a nice plump, round cheek by floating on the color in a semicircular motion. Allow the color to fade toward center without any line of demarcation. Wash on as many thin layers of warm white as needed to neutralize the background color. Keep these washes thin, and float shapes back if you find you are loosing detail. There should be value variation in the face, but no dead, dull background coming forward. These warm white washes can go right over the eye opening - just keep the color smooth and streak-free! Undercoat berries, jingle bells, apples, stars or other areas that need the color to be kept bright at the same time as you undercoat the face. **Buttermilk** is a good undercoating color. Build mouth colors along with the face tones. The light background or the off-white undercolor will provide a light glow on forward areas of the face. Whether you are painting Olde World Santas or more modern styles, the procedure is basically the same.

**PAINTING SKIN AREAS: Fleshtone - Medium Flesh - Shading Flesh - Brandy Wine/blush - Hiliting Flesh/for highlights**
**ILL. 2** **ALWAYS** let each layer of floated color dry thoroughly before proceeding to the next value. Working all areas help you establish balance. Begin by floating on the lightest skin value **(Fleshtone)** always blending your color out softly so that it disappears without a line of demarcation in toward the center of each area. Start by shaping the eyes in the same areas as for undercoating, correcting shape and size as needed. Float color on cheeks and on the tip of the nose keeping the three parts of the nose well defined. Float color on the sides and across the top of the forehead and shape the frontal area and the bridge of the nose.

**ILL.3** Begin light shading with **Medium Flesh.** Use this color to deepen the bottom outer areas of each cheek, the sides of the forehead and to sink the shadow in under the brow line and along against the bridge of the nose, softly fading away under the eye. Shade the nose tip and the outer side edges of the mouth.

**ILL. 4** Add more color in the same areas as for the Medium Flesh using **Shading Flesh.** Add some wrinkles across the forehead and perhaps on the cheek bone or on either side of the mouth (smile lines). I find Shading Flesh is a little too bright for my taste, so I add a few drops of bright green **(Dark Pine)** and shake the bottle well. Green is the complimentary color for red, so it will dull the color without deadening it. Do proceed slowly! A little goes a long way. The very deepest shadow areas are next to the bridge of the nose just under the brow. I brush-mix just a hint of **Russet** with my **Shading Flesh** for this.

**EYES :** Use **Charcoal Gray** to lightly lay in the upper lash-lines. Lightly draw in the bottom nose line with Shading Flesh if needed adding nostril openings at the same time with the Charcoal. Load a #2 flat shader for floating color with a soft blue like **Blue Mist**, then side-load for just a hair line of a **Blue Haze** along one side. Float in the blue eye color, keeping the darkest value along the out-side edge of the iris (IL. 2). Float in a pupil (IL. 3) with **Midnite Green** allowing it to remain a bit lighter in the middle area. Use the same color to add a shadow on the eye all the way across just beneath the upper eyelid. Eye shine is a dot of white in the upper half of each eye. Diagonally opposite the shine, lay a soft line (catch or reflected light ) of white along the edge of the pupil on the iris.
**BLUSH & HIGHLIGHTS - a very important finishing touch!** Add **Brandy Wine** blush on the cheeks, nose tip and perhaps just a hint on the bridge of the nose and up against the hair on the sides of the forehead. You'll need quite a lot of blush along the outer bottom sides of the cheeks and on the nose. Remember, it's cold on Christmas eve! Blend the floated color out softly.

This is the very last thing I do after all skin color and the eyes are totally completed. I use **Hiliting Flesh** for this. Begin by placing a dot of color on the center nose tip and blot with your finger tip. Repeat as needed until the nose has a nice shine. Lay a line of light down the center of the nose, but not all the way from top to bottom. Think forward areas, and add some shine on the cheekbones and in the center above and below just in the center of each eye on the very edge of the lashlines. If you've created wrinkles, highlight above the lines softly.

**BEARDS & HAIR:** Depending upon the background color, I use various shades of gray to fill the general hair areas . Do your hair while waiting for the various floated layers of skin color to dry. Load a flat shader for floating color in a light grey such as **Driftwood**. Brush-blend just a bit of **Neutral Gray** along the very edge of the brush filled for floating with the light gray value. Streak in the color following hairs directional flow. Get plenty of dark streaks in so that when you add white it will really show. Float a little **Charcoal Grey** just under the mustache and also wherever a strand of hair lays over another area. Using a **1/4-1/2" La Cornelle Filbert Rake,** stroke on the white to complete the hair (3), working each hair area separately. Color will need to be thinned enough to allow the bristles to separate and color to flow easily. Use a liner brush (4) with more thinned white to add the tiny wispy hairs and brows. Do several layers of the highlighting white until the beard really glows and the outer edges of the beard shape and or tips of the individual hairs are nice and soft.

I've done my very best to give you the progression of painting used for painting Santa faces my way. Nothing can replace a hands on painting experience where you can ask questions. If you feel you need more help, I've done two two-hour home video tapes illustrating painting Santa faces. One is done very basic, showing a lot about techniques, brush loading etc. along with a Santa face. The second reviews supplies, touches on stroke work & detailing and goes into detail with undercoating and painting a Santa face. I'm hoping to do a **Zawicki Tips & Techniques** video by spring '97 to help beginner painters as well as those who simply want to know more about my way of working with acrylic. Write for further information.

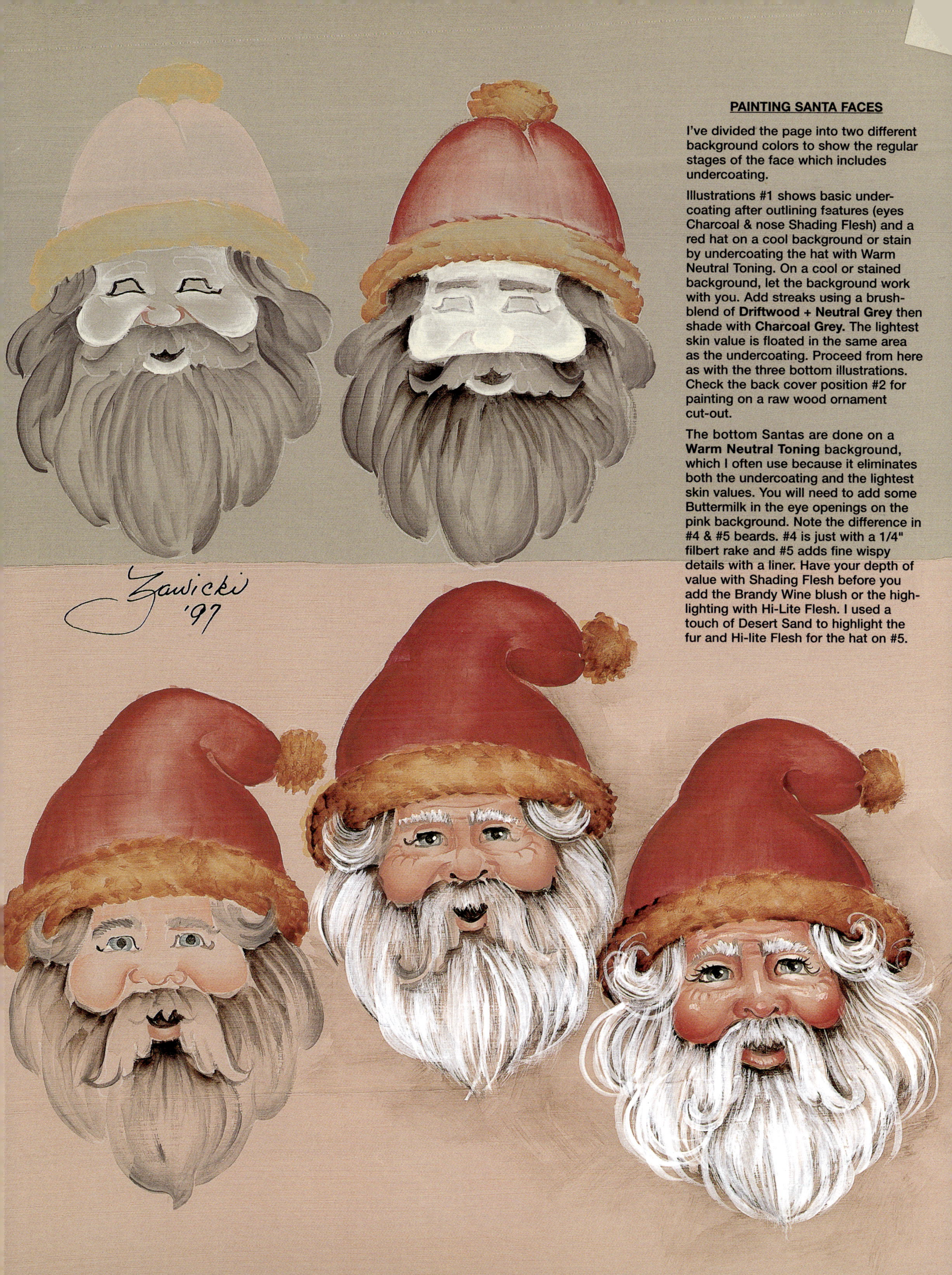

## PAINTING SANTA FACES

I've divided the page into two different background colors to show the regular stages of the face which includes undercoating.

Illustrations #1 shows basic undercoating after outlining features (eyes Charcoal & nose Shading Flesh) and a red hat on a cool background or stain by undercoating the hat with Warm Neutral Toning. On a cool or stained background, let the background work with you. Add streaks using a brush-blend of **Driftwood + Neutral Grey** then shade with **Charcoal Grey.** The lightest skin value is floated in the same area as the undercoating. Proceed from here as with the three bottom illustrations. Check the back cover position #2 for painting on a raw wood ornament cut-out.

The bottom Santas are done on a **Warm Neutral Toning** background, which I often use because it eliminates both the undercoating and the lightest skin values. You will need to add some Buttermilk in the eye openings on the pink background. Note the difference in #4 & #5 beards. #4 is just with a 1/4" filbert rake and #5 adds fine wispy details with a liner. Have your depth of value with Shading Flesh before you add the Brandy Wine blush or the high-lighting with Hi-Lite Flesh. I used a touch of Desert Sand to highlight the fur and Hi-lite Flesh for the hat on #5.

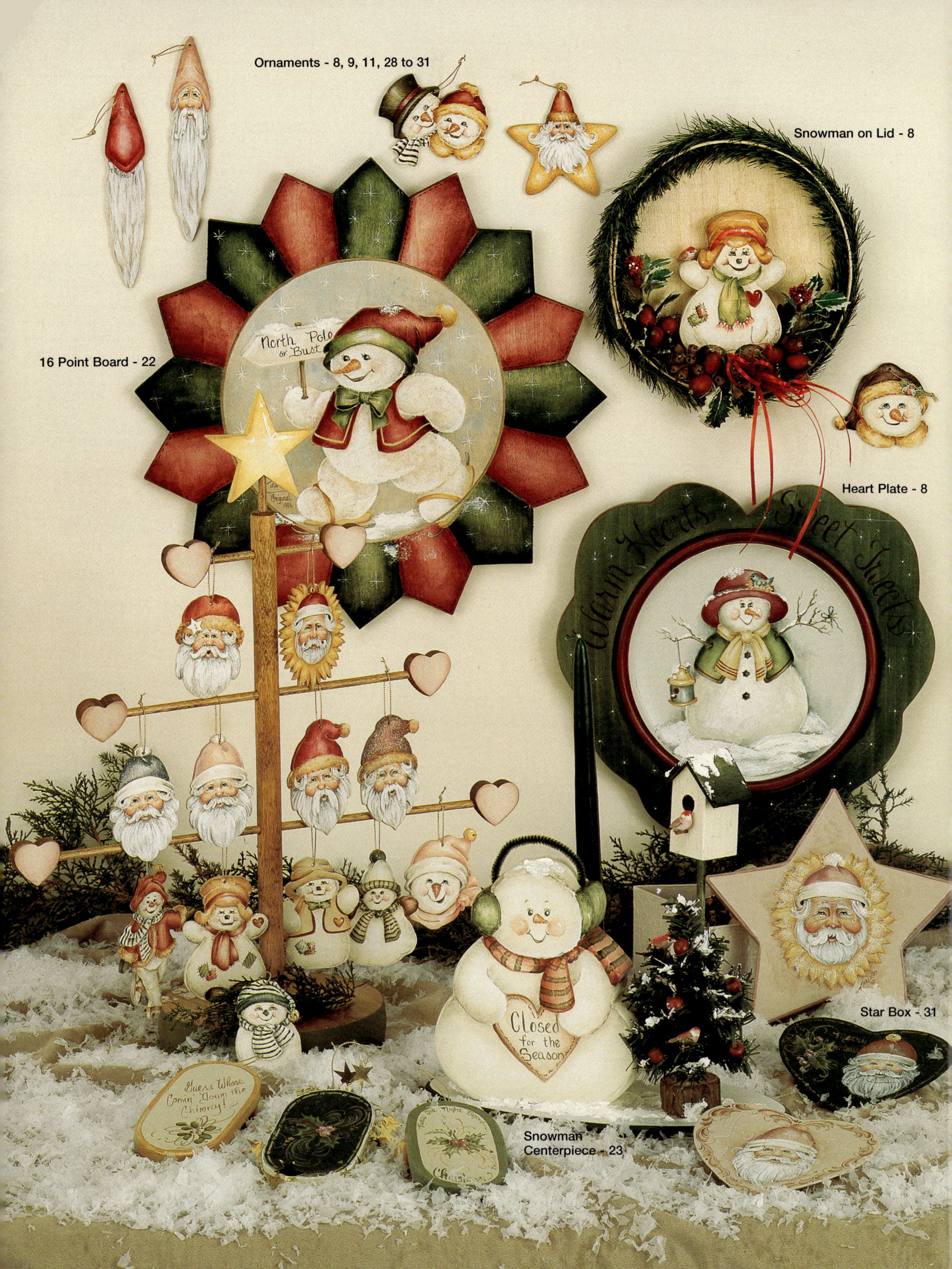


Ornaments - 8, 9, 11, 28 to 31

Snowman on Lid - 8

16 Point Board - 22

Heart Plate - 8

Star Box - 31

Snowman Centerpiece - 23

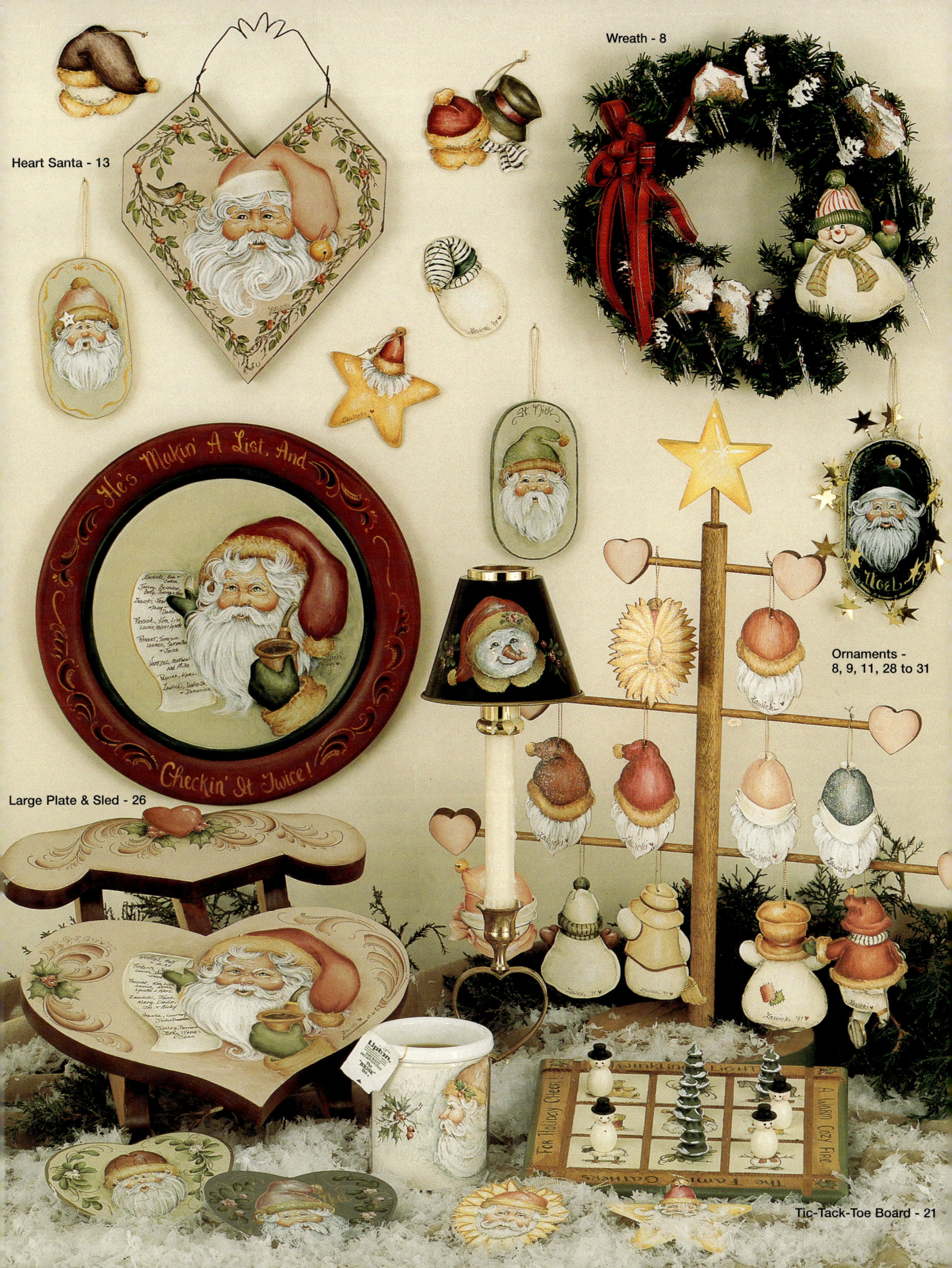


Heart Santa - 13

Wreath - 8

Ornaments - 8, 9, 11, 28 to 31

Large Plate & Sled - 26

Tic-Tack-Toe Board - 21

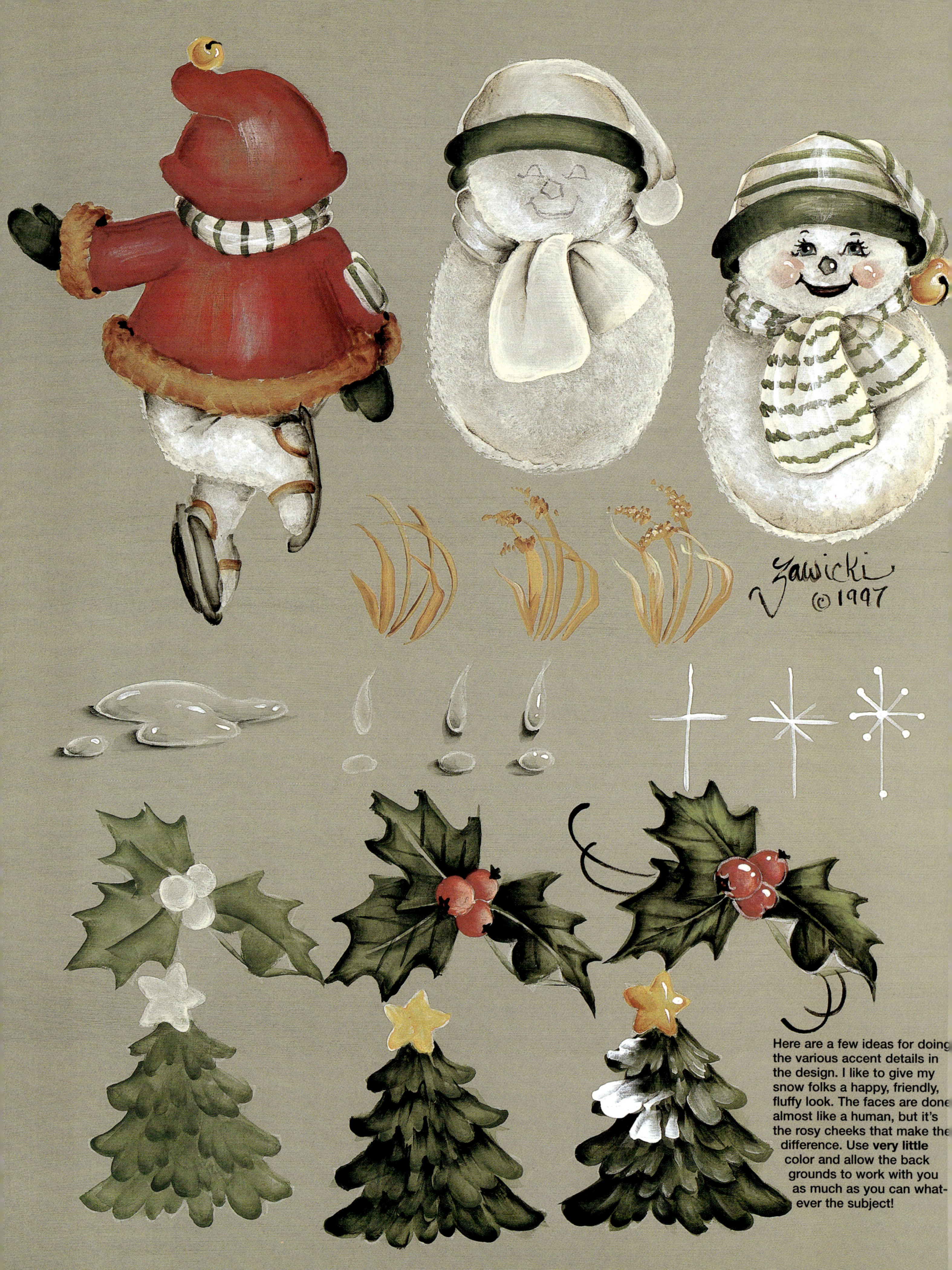


Here are a few ideas for doing the various accent details in the design. I like to give my snow folks a happy, friendly, fluffy look. The faces are done almost like a human, but it's the rosy cheeks that make the difference. Use **very little** color and allow the back grounds to work with you as much as you can whatever the subject!

**LETS PAINT A SNOWMAN!** If you're a snowman fan and have done lots of snowmen, you may want to just continue with whatever techniques you've enjoyed working with in the past. I've worked with several different techniques over time, but I think I get the job done best as follows. Outline facial feathures with **Charcoal Grey**. I like to get a little soft textured effect, and to do this quickly I like to use a **"Deer Foot Stippler"**. Loew-Cornell makes them in several sizes, as do a number of other brush manufacturer's. Select one that is tight and compact and with a relatively short bristle length so the bristles will not bend over as you stipple. Use the largest brush you can to save time, but if you only buy one, let it be a smaller size. I trace on the facial details right away, then do the snow areas. The outline of the eyes and mouth with Charcoal and the nose with Russet still shows through, even if some of the stippling goes over them. Facial details are darkened after the base color and shading is in place. I use a liner and usually **Charcoal Grey** to outline the eyes, add lashes and for the mouth shape. If the mouth is slightly open, add **Russet + Charcoal** in the opening. Noses are often carrots. Use a liner and **Russet** to outline and add the little ridges on the carrots. I then brush-blend a little **Brandy Win**e into some **Golden Straw** to make the orange color. Noses can also be a chunk of coal. Do this with **Midnite Green** floating the color for value variation. I lightly float shading over the stippled on **Buttermilk** with **Charcoal Grey** or a blend of **Charcoal Grey + Midnite Green**. Leave a soft haze of the Buttermilk along the curved edges of the figures as a reflected light. Keep shading very soft on snow folks, pulling the shadow of the snow beneath it in with the shading on the rounded bottoms of the snowman's shape. Highlight forward areas with white, giving special highlighting above and below the center of the eyes, on the cheeks, chin, and around the mouth. The cheeks are floated in with just a hint of **Brandy Wine**, but don't make a complete circle of color. Highlight the cheeks with white.

I often give my snow folks eyes that are like a humans. Create the iris with **Blue Mist** shadeding the outside edge with **Blue Haze**. I use **Midnite Green** for the pupils. Put in a strong shine of white, then add a reflected light against the pupil on the iris of the eye diagonally opposite the strong shine dot. If I do a dot eye, it can be either Midnite Green or Charcoal Grey. Give the eyes tiny Charcoal eyelashes after you have highlighted the snow above and below center on the eye with white.

If you like, "Real Snow" texture can be softly poked on with a small flat (old is good) brush using **SNOW-TEX**. Apply the texture after all shadows are in place, and try not to cover all shading. I also put bits of texture on other horizontal or semi-horizontal surfaces to balance the texture. If you like a bit of glitz you can cover the snow areas and the snow folks themselves with **Heavy Metal GLIMMER Clear** if you wish. I kind of like the way it makes the snow sparkle like real life, but it's a matter of personal taste.

Dressing your snow folks is a matter of personal color preference. I've not wasted space to give you every color for every version I've painted. Look at the color photographs, then go to your paints and find something similar. You will want to have at least two compatible colors. One for the main color to be floated in, leaving more sheer areas for a lighter value and the other a darker value to give you a chance for deeper shading. Highlight with a light value or white. Adding your own special little details like patches, hearts, wiggly lines, holly or other berries with stroke leaves, etc. will give a lot of originality to your work. I've shown the back view of the skating snowman so you'll have a pattern. It's the hardest one to figure out. For other backs, match up areas with outer edge contours and wrap appropriate color around to the back.

<u>SEA OATS:</u> These are done by simply drawing in the main stem with a liner. You can use any soft golden tone for them. Either **Yellow Ochre** or **Golden Straw** tipped into **Raw Sienna** is fine. Draw fine lines for the stem, then apply varied pressure with the liner to create the long leaves that go with the oat stems. At the ends of the oat stems I just dot on color to create a seed head. Remember that the winds blow by the sea, so bend the stems all in the same direction. Highlight with a touch of **Taffy Cream**.

<u>TEAR/WATER DROPS & PUDDLES:</u> This is one of those times where less is more. Water is transparent, so is painted more as an illusion. It's a bit of shadow and some hard shines, with a hint of reflected light on edges. Use a very small flat shader (#1 or 2) and side-load into **Buttermilk** or a color of the surface the water i s on. VERY SOFTLY float in the shape of the water, but don't make a completely solid outline. Now place a shadow under the bottom left area of the water using a dull, dark value of the surface color. Place a lighter shadow inside the water area at the lower left with the same color. Now add a hard shine of white on the upper right and you're done! KEEP IT SIMPLE!!!

<u>SNOWFLAKES:</u> You could get really carried away,but I'm lazy so I begin with a long vertical line, the cross it with a horizontal line that is slightly shorter. Place two diagonal lines that are shorter still and dot the center with a dip-dot of the same white color. Add connecting lines or dots at the ends of the lines with more dip-dots if you're ambitious!

<u>HOLLY & BERRIES:</u> I float in the shape of the berries with a light pink or off-white depending on the background or color I'm heading toward. I then float in the out shapes of the leaves with **Lt. Avocado** blending in toward the middle of the leaf, allow to dry then wash lightly with the same color. Leave an absence of color down the middle of the leaf for a center vein. Slide on the chisel edge of the brush to create the side veins. Shade the leaves with **Plantation Pine** for the forward leaves of the cluster and **Evergreen** over the Plantation for leaves further back in the cluster. Add a splash of sunshine in forward areas with some **Olive Green**.

To complete the berries, I float the shape with a red like **Brandy Wine** (sh/Cranberry Wine) or perhaps **Mauve** (sh/Brandy Wine) for a pink berry, blending softly in toward the middle using a small flat shader. Keep the paint more sheer in the upper right to create a soft highlighted forward area. Your hard white shines will be added over this area last. Shade the berries on the bottom left or when one tucks behind another. Add some blossom ends with a liner and **Midnite Green**. Add reflected light around berries to set the apart for each other and the rest of the area and also around the blossom ends usually with **Hi-lite Flesh**.

<u>CHRISTMAS TREES:</u> I use basically the same colors as for holly or other leaves. I shape with medium value beginning at the bottom, wash, then shade under branches. Add highlight with perhaps **Jade Green** or lay on drifts of snow with white and a large flat shader.

***For his body & features*** *follow basic Snowman instructions on page #19.*

**HAT BAND, BANNER & SCARF:** Float in the areas of these shapes and Stipple in the pom-pom with **Buttermilk**. Shade with predominantly **Midnite Green** brush-mixing in a bit of **Blue Haze** here and there, especially on the banner. Highlight with white.

The Stripes, fringe, border and lettering of the banner are done with slightly thinned **Russet** using a fine liner. Do the little hearts on the hat band with **Brandy Wine** shaded with **Russet**.

**MITTENS & HAT:** Use **Avocado Lt.** shaded with **Evergreen** and highlighted with **Jade Green**.

Use **Charcoal Grey** highlighted with **Buttermilk** for the branch arms.

# LITTLE SAMMY SNOWMAN

Use a 9 1/2 x 12 1/2" blackboard or reduce the design enough to fit the board you have.

The wood edge is painted with **Buttermilk**. The easiest way to do the little trees is to cut a triangle stencil and stencil in the main tree shape with **Lt. Avocado** with a petifour sponge. Float in shading of **Evergreen** and add **Charcoal Grey** trunks with a liner. The wavy line and trio of dip-dots are done with **Russet** as is the lettering.
(See page 28 for border)

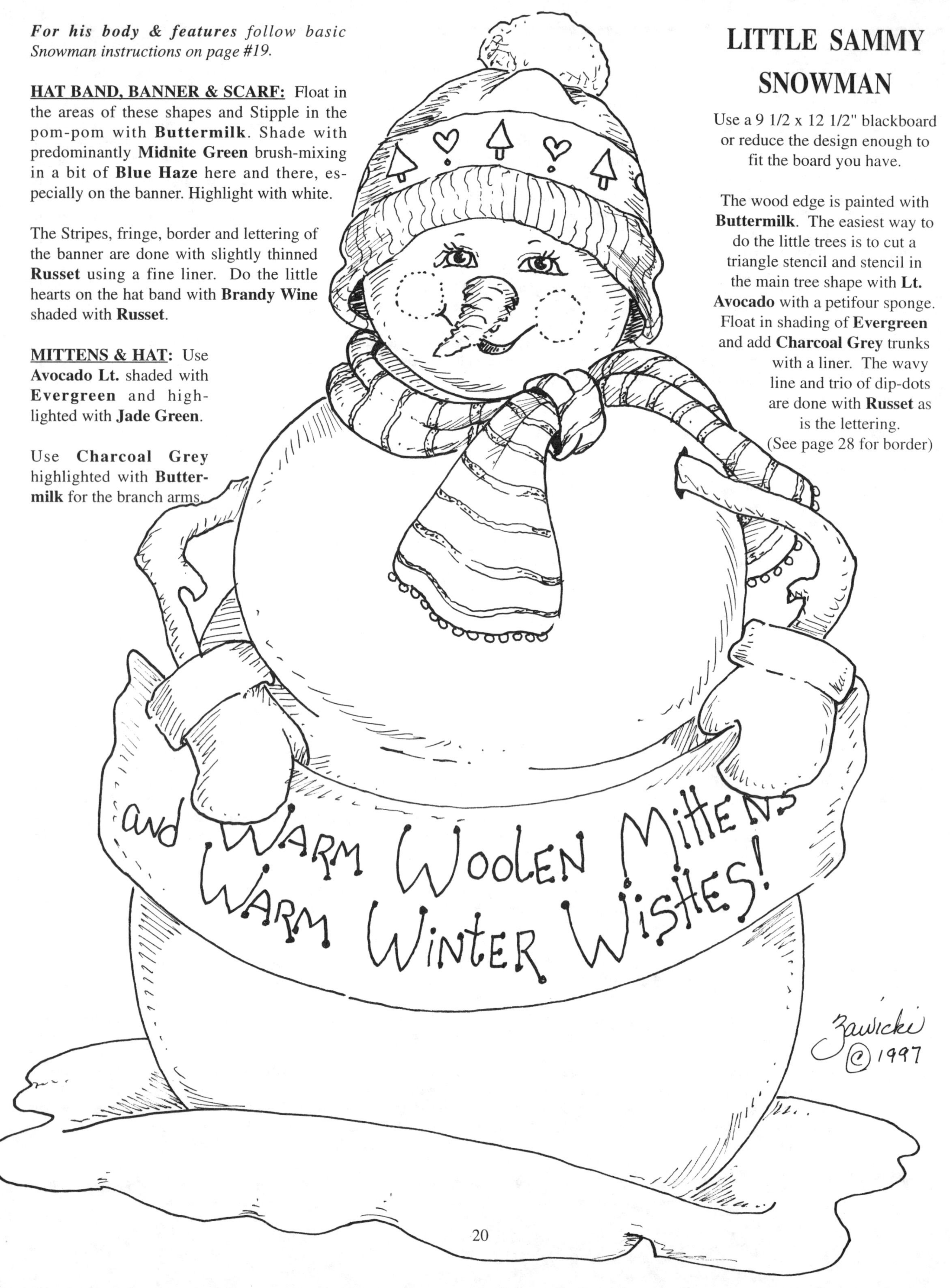

## TIC-TACK-TOE For Family Fun!

*I love having toys around at Christmas under the tree or on the coffee table even though my kids are grown and gone! Cut from 1" pine stock, the spaces between the squares have been dadoed out so the centers and edges are raised about 1/8".*

Sand then stain the entire tic-tack-toe board Minwax Puritan Pine. Apply **Avocado Lt.** around the outer edge with a petifour sponge and **Buttermilk** on the raised squares of the board. I've done these boards with all different themes. This one is for Christmas and you can cut tree and snowman playing pieces also cut from 1" pine stock or find little turnings as I have. Trace on the design shapes with white graphite, then go over the lines with a Micron PIGMA size 01 pen. Add a few of the shading details with the pen. It will now go very quickly to lightly fill in colors and add just a hint of shading as needed with your acrylic paint. The lettering around the edge is done with a liner and **Charcoal Grey.** **Browns -** Yellow Ochre, Raw Sienna & Milk Chocolate. **Golds -** Golden Straw & Honey Brown. **Greens -** Avo-cado Lt.& Plantation Pine. **Greys/Blacks -** Driftwood, Neutral Grey, Charcoal Grey & Midnite Green. **Reds -** Brandy Wine & Cranberry Wine. The corner holly squares are painted with traditional techniques. Varnish & enjoy!

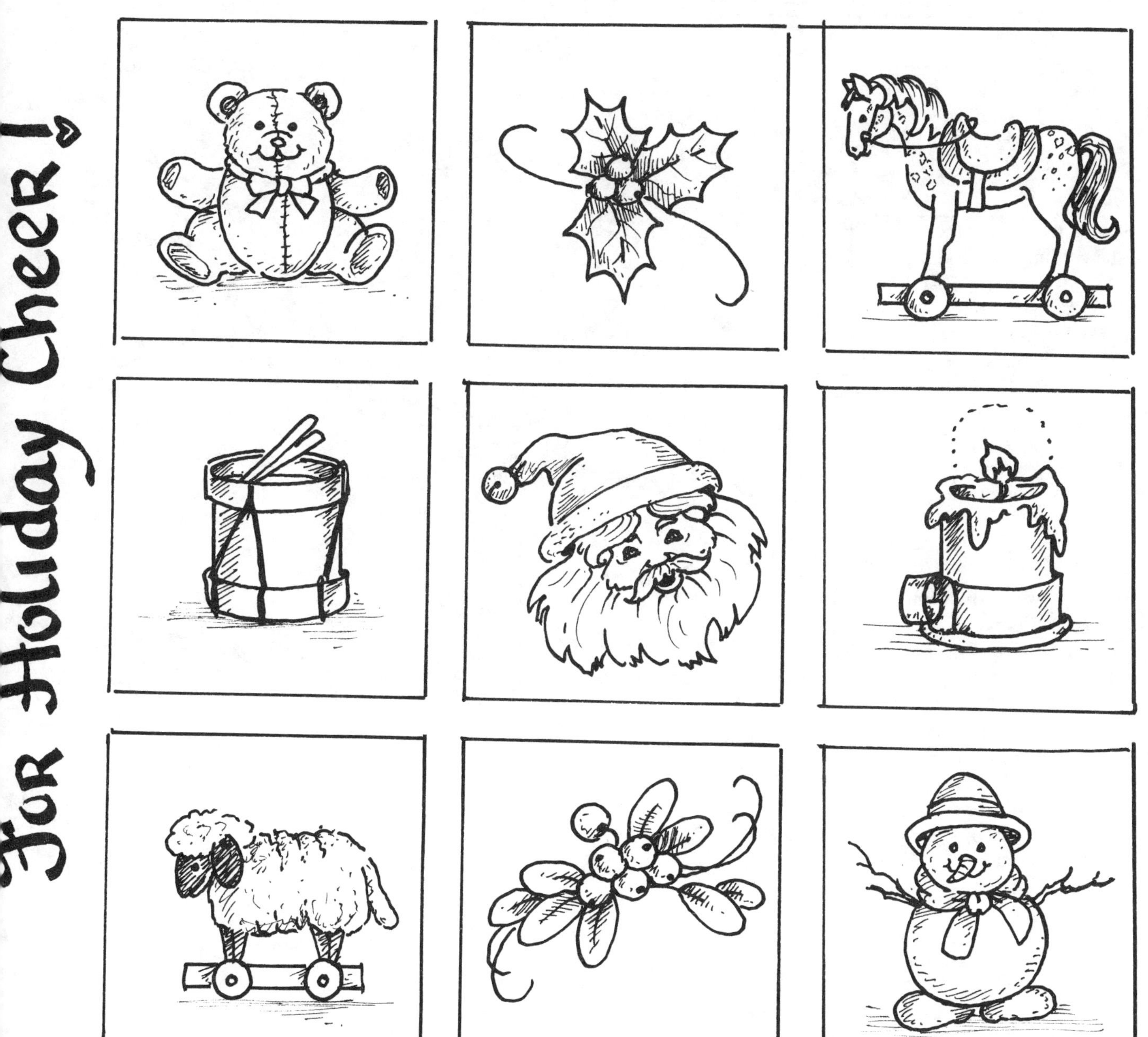

# Skatin' Along!

*This is a board I had cut from 1/2" baltic birch. The shape is from a quilt block design. It was painted on raw wood, so you can just trace the design with white graphite.*

**INNER CIRCLE BACKGROUND:** Apply a slightly thinned coat of color in a slip-slap manner over the background around the figure using a 1/2" wash brush. Begin with **Dove Grey**. At random, brush-blend in a hint of **Blue Mist, Blue Haze & Buttermilk**. The object is to obtain a soft grey atmospheric effect for the background color.

**TIE, HAT BAND & GREEN OUTER EDGE POINTS:**
The points are floated in with a 1/2" wash brush, leaving the centers with less color so they remain lighter. I used **Evergreen** for the points, and **Lt. Avocado** shaded with the **Evergreen** for the tie and hat band.

**VEST AND HAT and SKATES:**
Use **Burgundy Wine** floated on to establish the shapes of the hat and vest. Shade with a hint of **Black Plum**. The tassel on the hat, the skate bottoms and straps and the cording on the vest were done with **Yellow Ochre**. Shade the tassel and skates with **Raw Sienna**. Use **Charcoal Grey** lightly to create the blades on the skates. Highlight with **Buttermilk**.

I also used the Burgundy for alternating points around the outer edge.

**THE SIGN:**
Float in the shape with **Buttermilk**. Shade with a hint of **Raw Sienna**. Lettering is done with **Charcoal Grey**. The pole is **Raw Sienna** shaded with **Charcoal**.

**SNOWFLAKES**: Using a liner, do a long vertical then a horizontal line with white. Place two shorter lines diagonally through the first crossed lines. A dot of color can be placed in the center intersection if desired. Vary sizes of the flakes.

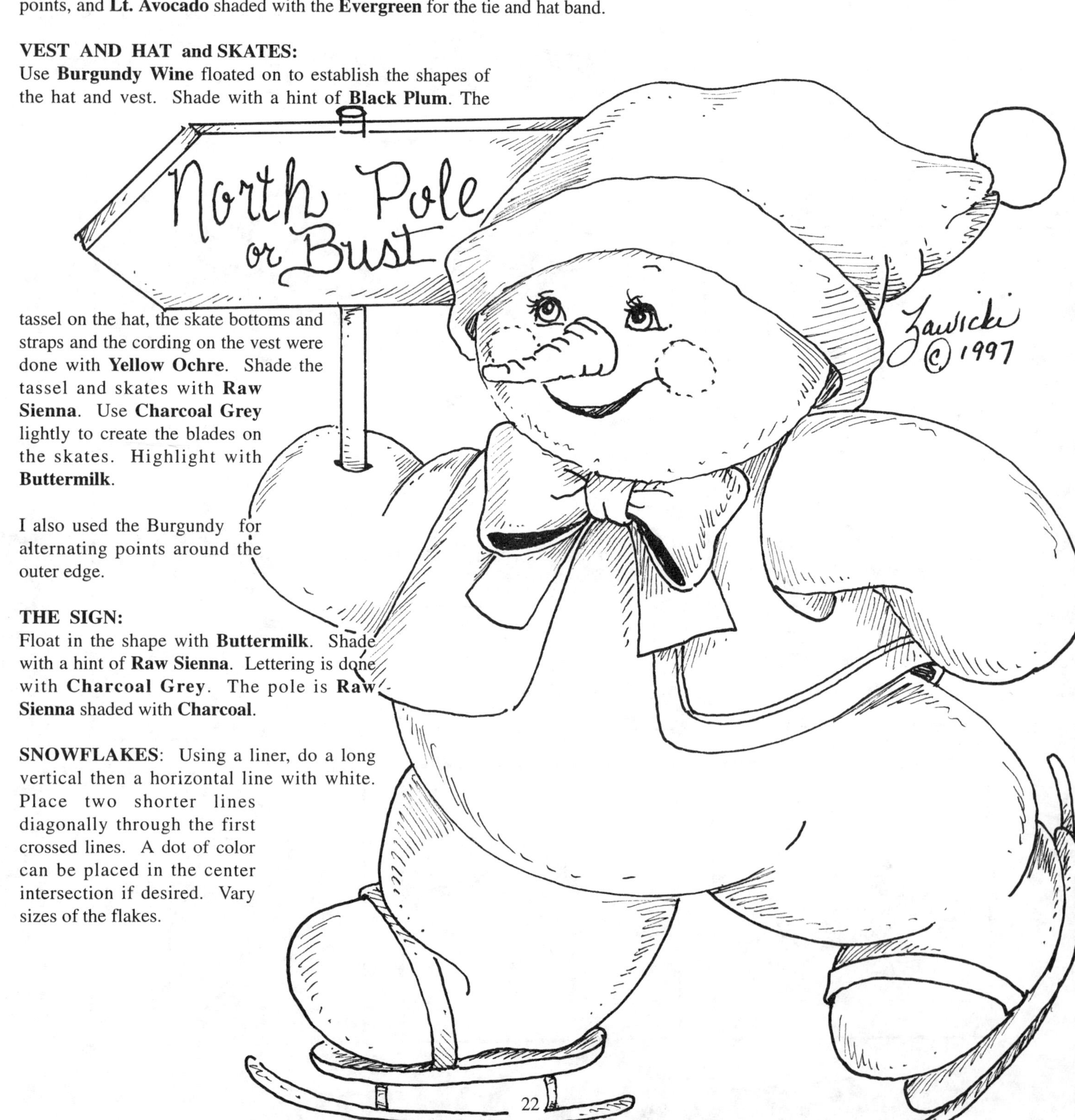

# SNOWMAN CENTERPIECE

***This little unit would be great as a centerpiece, or on a buffet table all through the winter! It's easy enough even for beginners too. Add more candles for an even more festive effect!***

The snowman was cut from 2" pine stock, and was slightly rounded along the edges. The little birdhouse is cut from a 1 1/4" wide, 1 1/2" deep piece of pine with an angled top as shown below. Add some thin wood 1 3/4" wide for a roof with a slight overhang. Drill a small hole and insert a bit of moss. Add a tiny dowel for a perch and mount it on a 1/4" dowel. Position the snowman, drill a hole for the birdhouse. OPTION: Position a candle cup so it is slightly behind both.

Apply two liberal coats of **Buttermilk** to the entire snowman and also for the main part of the birdhouse. Paint the roof of the birdhouse with **Evergreen**, slightly thinned. I used the same color for the pole of the birdhouse and the candle cup. Trace a suggestion of the arms where they meet against the heart he holds, the heart and just the middle section of the scarf. Because of the shape of the wood, you will want to use your chalk pencil to extend any lines to the edges of the wood where little changes in the contour would indicate. Otherwise, arms and other areas don't necessarily end up exactly where they should.

To do the ear muffs, I lightly fluffed in **Plantation Pine**. Allow the background to become the light value. By the time you've finished the second side, you can go back to the first and begin adding another layer of the same color for shading.
The scarf is floated in with **Brandy Wine**. Shade it with **Russet** then add some stripes with the **Plantation Pine** using a #4 flat shader. The heart he holds is floated in with **Warm Neutral Toning** and shaded with **Russet**. Use the **Plantation Pine** for the lettering and **Russet** for the squiggly trim around the edge of the heart. I also applied **Russet** around the top edge of the candle cup.

For the back, very little shaping is needed. Bring the scarf around where the neck would be and of course in the area that extends beyond the curve of the arm shape. Note the little dash line indications for the body shape in the back, add the ear muffs and that's about all you need.

Poke a little hole above the ear muffs with an awl and glue in a length of chenille stem. Glue or screw your other pieces in place on the 5 1/2x11" base painted **Dove Grey**. Add **Snow-Tex** with a palette knife, adding **Glamour Dust** if you like. Or, how about creating a "Memory Box" (from Wayne) by simply changing the message on the heart. Paint page edge **Buttermilk** and do a vignette area the color of your choice over any stain. I've sponged **Yellow Ochre** then **Desert Sand** over **Puritan Pine** stain. Add a few veins of **Buttermilk** with a wedge brush.

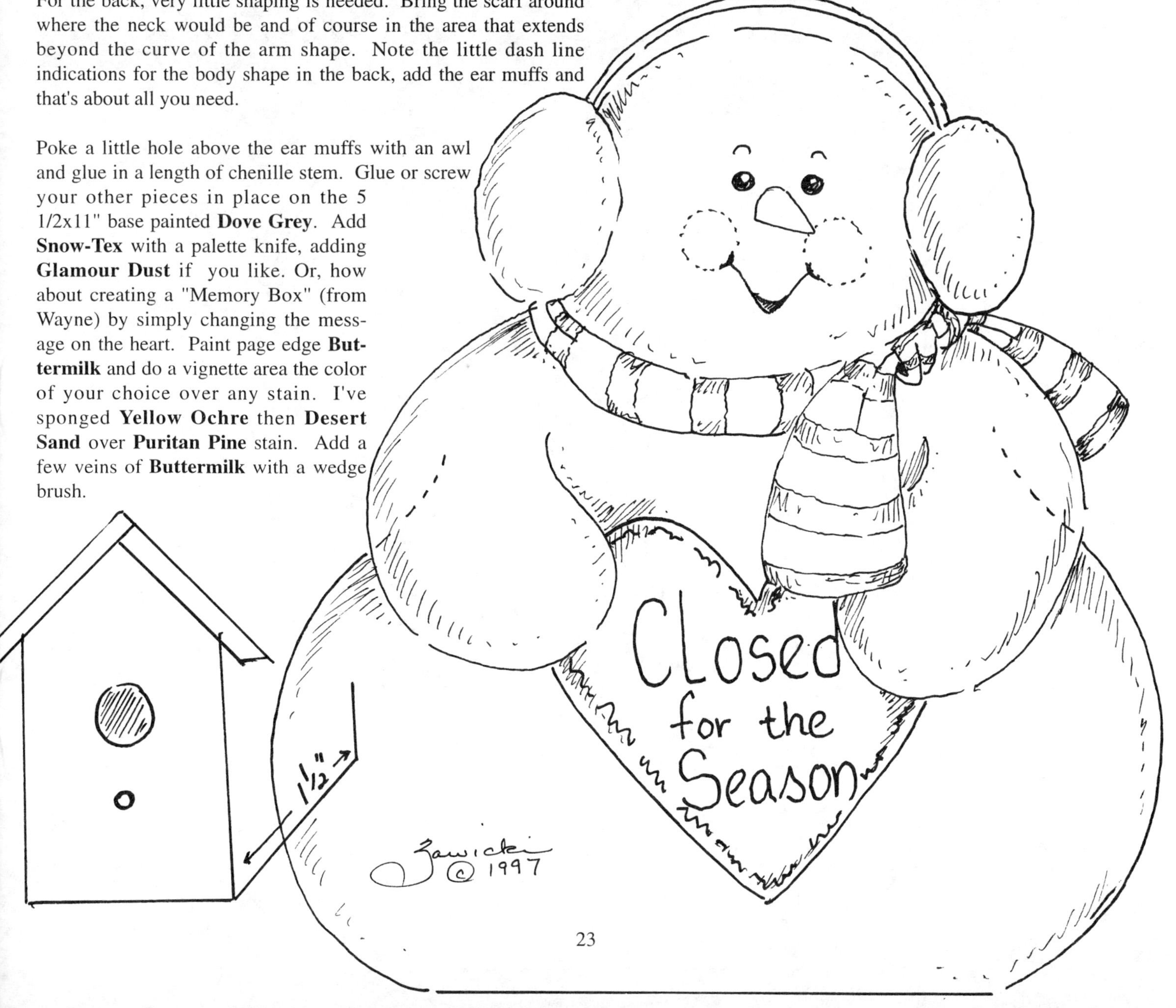

# SNOW ANGEL

*Here is another fast & easy project! I've given you a bottom line for a wreath cut-out (rounded) or a sitting bottom. Try both wood and fabric wings for this little sweetie. Accessory possibilities are limitless!!!*

**PREPARATION:** There is a **Brandy Wine** heart shaded with **Cranberry Wine** on her breast. Wings are based in **Driftwood** then light values are floated in to for little rounded feather tips and an outside edge first with **Dove Grey** then with **Buttermilk**. A bit of **Neutral Grey** shading can be added. The hair is a bit of **Spanish Moss** and the halo a piece of **Star Garland**. Add a double circle of **tinsel garland** for a wreath. Hot glue on a few little **dried rose buds** and **a bow** in the colors of your choice. Hang her alone in a wall grouping or wire her on a wreath, adding more star garland, icicle garland pieces, snow flakes or whatever! If you wish, create wings of fabric by adding a 1/4" seam allowance to the wing pattern. Cut two, perhaps of the gold stars on white background fabric, sandwich a couple layers of fluffy batting between the layers, sew a seam then pink out the shape. Glue to the back of the wood cut-out. Just let your imagination GO!!! She's easy enough to do one for everyone on your gift list. Note: I've used a chunk of coal for a nose on this one.

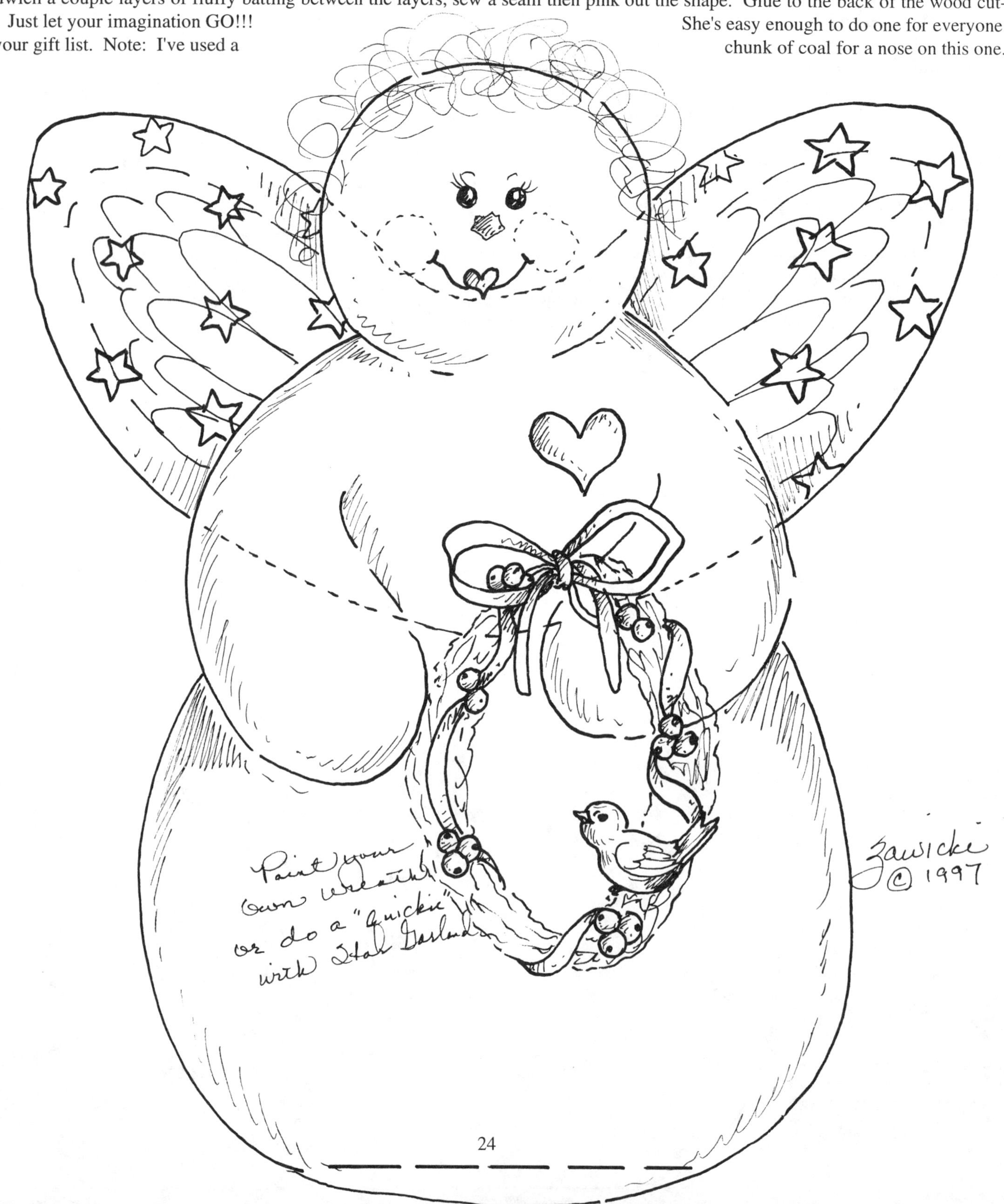

# SOUTHBOUND!

*He tried so hard to make it all the way to Florida, but that southern sun did SnowBoy in! This project, done on a 12" Bentwood box, and is dedicated to all my painting friends in Florida.*

I gave the top of the box a couple generous coats of **Ice Blue**. Trace on your design with white graphite. Use a **Pigma Micron** size **.01** pen from Sakura to do the lettering and some detailing. I kept my colors soft. The piece can be left out indefinitely to hold pens, paper, little treasures, etc. for handy access.

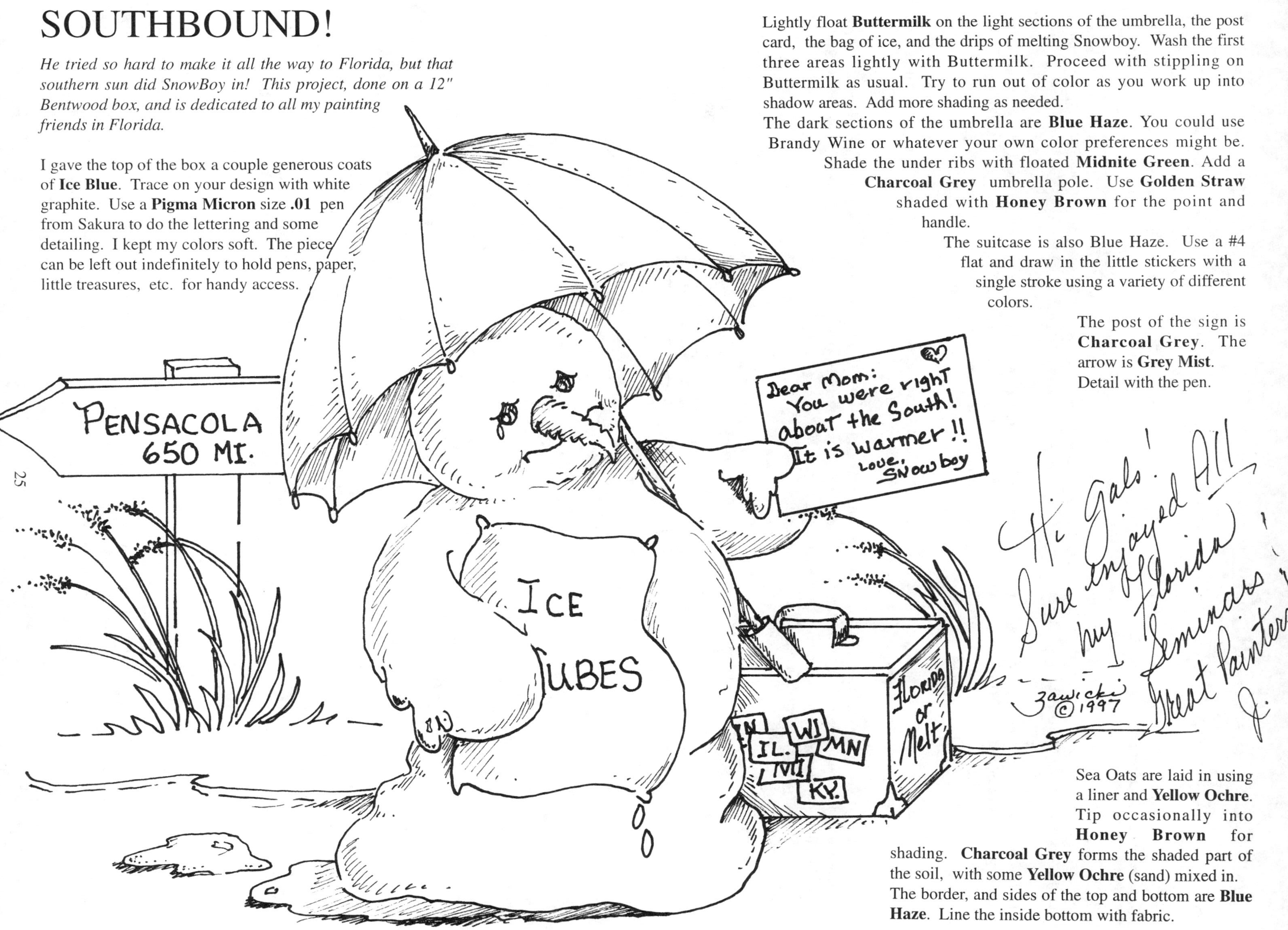


Lightly float **Buttermilk** on the light sections of the umbrella, the post card, the bag of ice, and the drips of melting Snowboy. Wash the first three areas lightly with Buttermilk. Proceed with stippling on Buttermilk as usual. Try to run out of color as you work up into shadow areas. Add more shading as needed.

The dark sections of the umbrella are **Blue Haze**. You could use Brandy Wine or whatever your own color preferences might be. Shade the under ribs with floated **Midnite Green**. Add a **Charcoal Grey** umbrella pole. Use **Golden Straw** shaded with **Honey Brown** for the point and handle.

The suitcase is also Blue Haze. Use a #4 flat and draw in the little stickers with a single stroke using a variety of different colors.

The post of the sign is **Charcoal Grey**. The arrow is **Grey Mist**. Detail with the pen.

Sea Oats are laid in using a liner and **Yellow Ochre**. Tip occasionally into **Honey Brown** for shading. **Charcoal Grey** forms the shaded part of the soil, with some **Yellow Ochre** (sand) mixed in. The border, and sides of the top and bottom are **Blue Haze**. Line the inside bottom with fabric.

# SANTA COOKIE PLATE
## or Heart Sled

*I love these plates with the inner bead! They are great for adding a little accent of color. I've done the design on a sled also. Both are from* **Wayne's Woodenware***. This design would look great on a round box . . . or almost anything you like!*

**THE PLATE:** Moisten the outside rim with water, then apply slightly thinned **Cranberry Wine** with a 1/2" wash brush for best area control. Now apply thinned color with a sponge to the back of the plate so that the wood grain still shows through. I did the center with solid **Cool Neutral Toning**. The bead was carefully painted with a #6 flat shader and **Evergreen**.

Follow page 14 for the Santa face and beard. I used **Cranberry Wine** for the hat and **Evergreen** for the mittens. Use **Yellow Ochre** shading with **Raw Sienna** and **Dark Chocolate** for the bowl and wide area of the stem of the pipe. Use **Golden Straw** shaded with **Raw Sienna** for the small band and **Charcoal Grey** shaded with **Midnite Green** for the rest of the stem. Background shadows around the figure are **Midnite Green**.

The list is floated in with **Buttermilk** then shaded with a brush-mix of **Charcoal & Midnite Green**. Highlight with **White** then do the names of your choice with a liner and Charcoal or a Pigma MICRON pen.

**THE SLED:** The entire sled was stained with Puritan Pine. **Warm Neutral Toning**. was applied on the entire top surface. I then sketched in the shape of the little heart with a chalk pencil, then floated **Brandy Wine** on the heart. Shade with a touch of **Russet**. The thickness edges of the sled were painted **Russet** using a **Petifour Sponge** and a flat brush in small areas. Trace on the design with white graphite. Old friends know this is my favorite Santa background color! You can totally skip the undercoating and lightest skin value steps and begin with the **Medium Flesh**! Follow instructions on page 14 for painting the design. I used a blend of **Charcoal Grey** with just a hint of **Russet** for background shadows on the sled. Background between the hat tassel and the cuff should have hat color faded away as you move out away from the design. I used **Brandy Wine** shaded with **Cranberry Wine** for the hat and **Lt. Avocado** shaded with **Plantation Pine** for mittens. If you wish, a bit of strokework using a #10 flat and some **Russet** detailed with a liner and **Charcoal Grey** or **Evergreen**. I often use a bit of strokework to fill in negative space on various pro-jects. It takes a bit of practice, but is well worth it in the long run. Once you master the techniques, it be-comes a really fast and easy way to fill in areas without lengthy painting or added design.

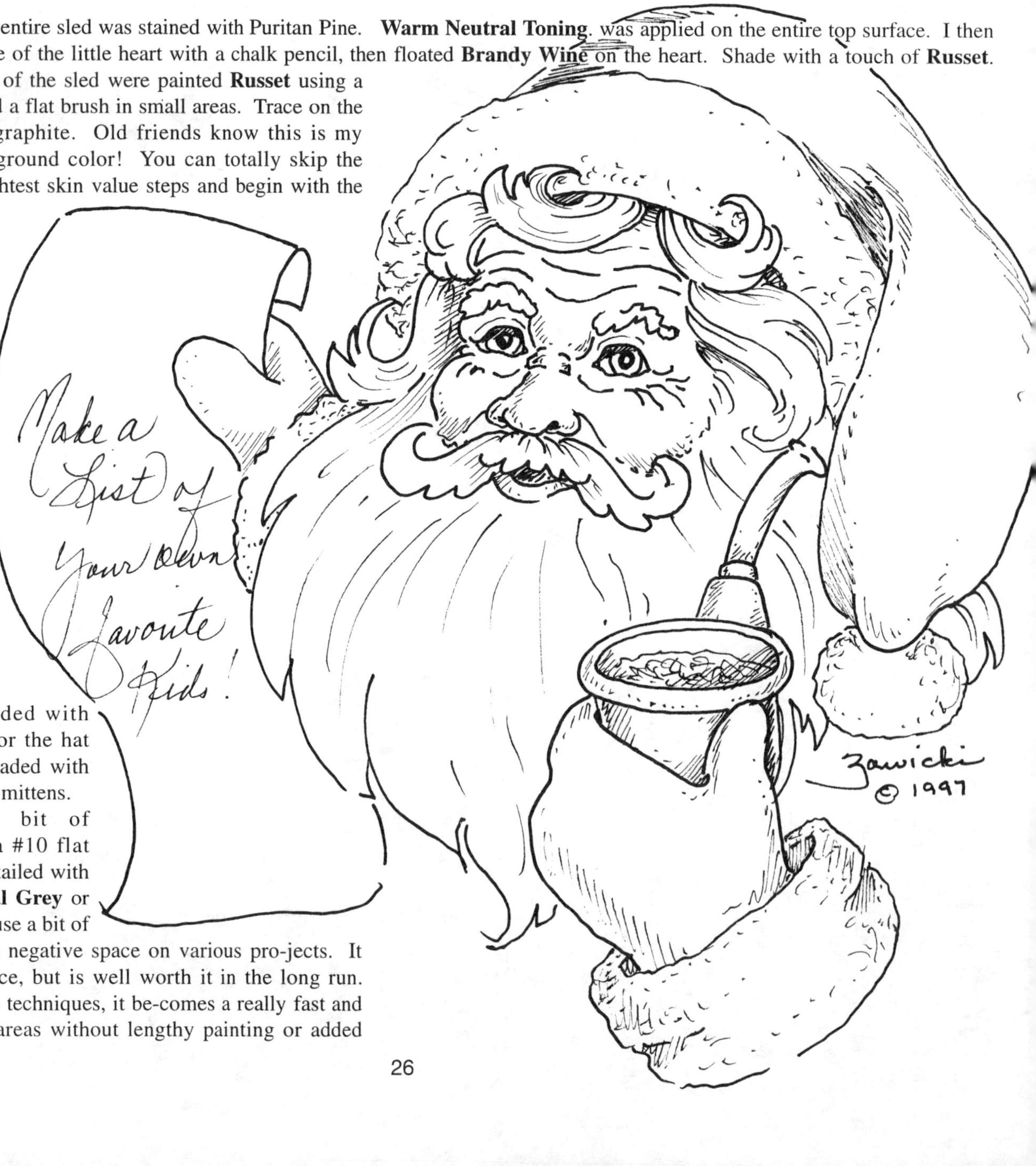

# Strokework For The Santa With a List Sled

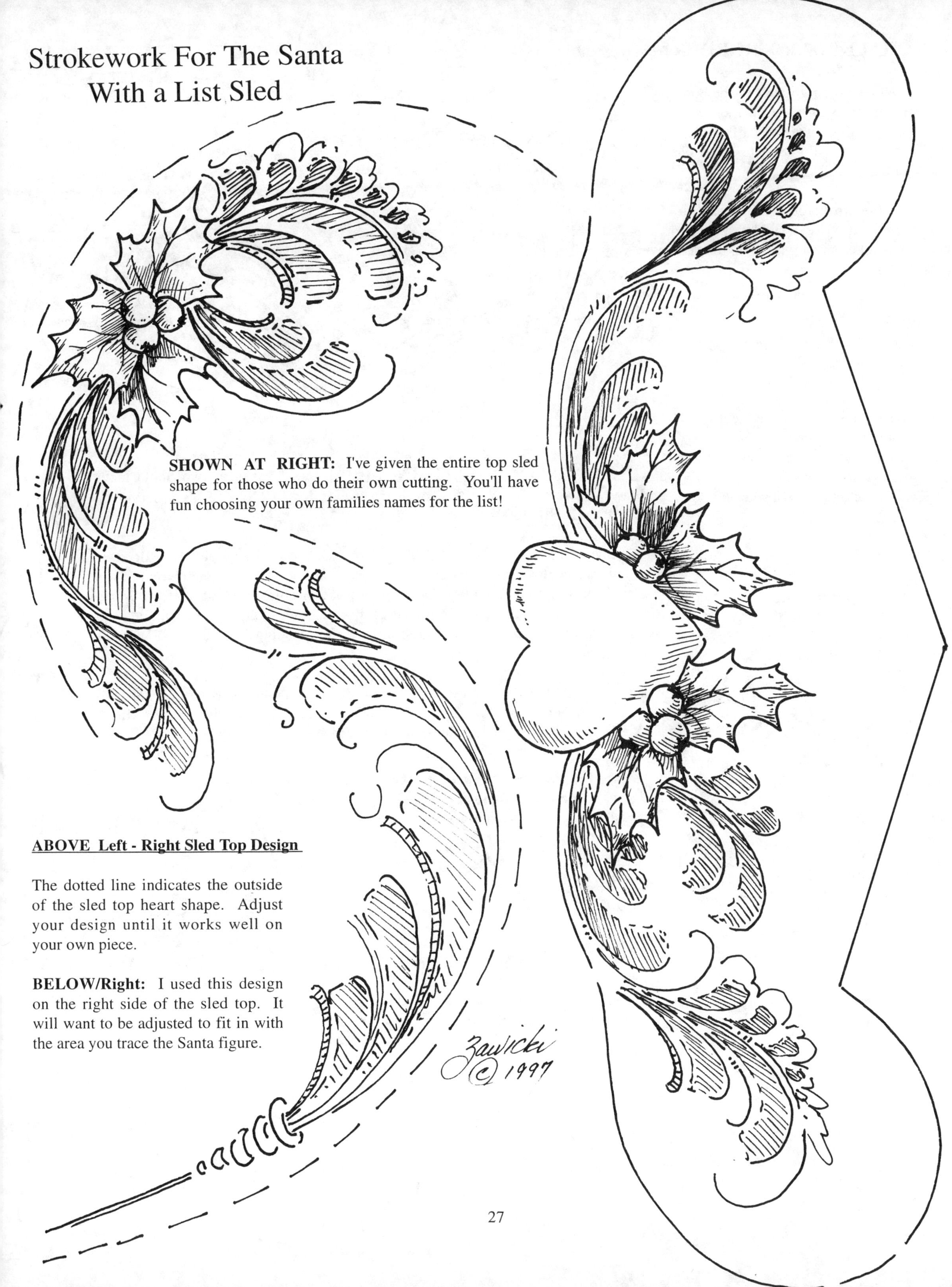


**SHOWN AT RIGHT:** I've given the entire top sled shape for those who do their own cutting. You'll have fun choosing your own families names for the list!

**ABOVE Left - Right Sled Top Design**

The dotted line indicates the outside of the sled top heart shape. Adjust your design until it works well on your own piece.

**BELOW/Right:** I used this design on the right side of the sled top. It will want to be adjusted to fit in with the area you trace the Santa figure.

## CHALKBOARD BORDER from page 20

I've given the right half of the border if you wish to trace on the design. Reverse to get the left half. I used a stylus for the dip-dot trios and a liner for the curved stroke.

Try the stroke design at right on a glass ball. Use a #6 flat shader for the strokes and a liner to do the detail lines.

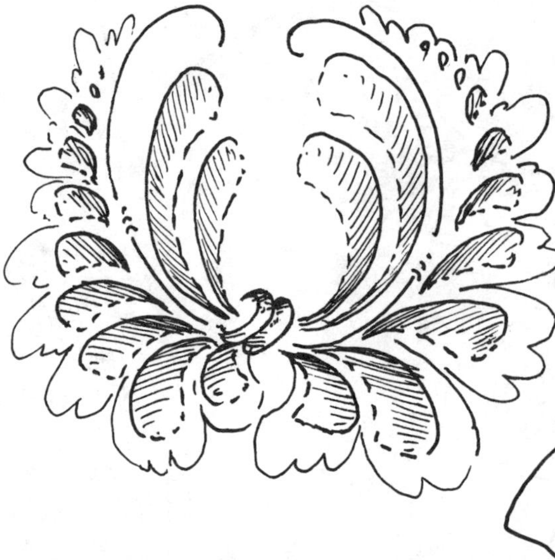

**TOP HAT SNOWMAN**
Pg. 9

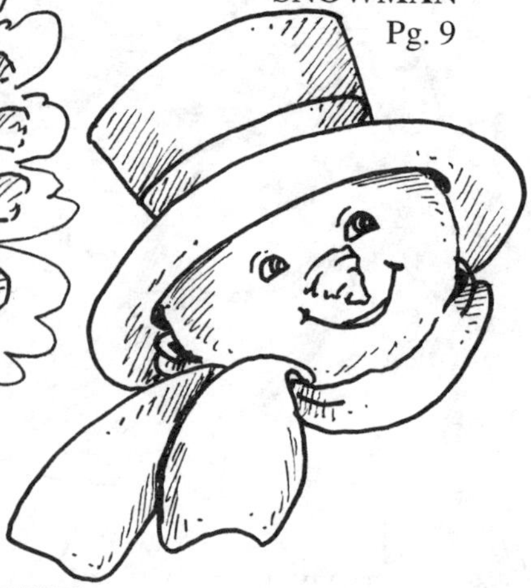

This is the size of the snowman from page 30 that was used for an ornament cut-out. I traced just the head, hat & scarf for use on one of the glass balls. See page 18 for the back view.

**PAINT A SATIN BALL ORNAMENT** I used two Santa faces and two snowmen for on the beautiful satin finish **ORNAMENTS** from the **ARTIST'S CLUB**. (800-

Trace only the most strategic parts. The curve makes large tracing areas difficult so trace only the central important areas. You may want to sketch vague extremities in with a chalk pencil for a guide. Don't over-stroke or color lifts; allow extra drying time between layers of color; basecoat each area completely before shading and highlighting; press excess water from brushes before loading with acrylic. Work as you would on any non-porous surface.

When finished, allow the paint to cure several hours then apply several light mists of mat spray or use a brush-on waterbase varnish just over painted portions. The reduced designs used are shown on his page.

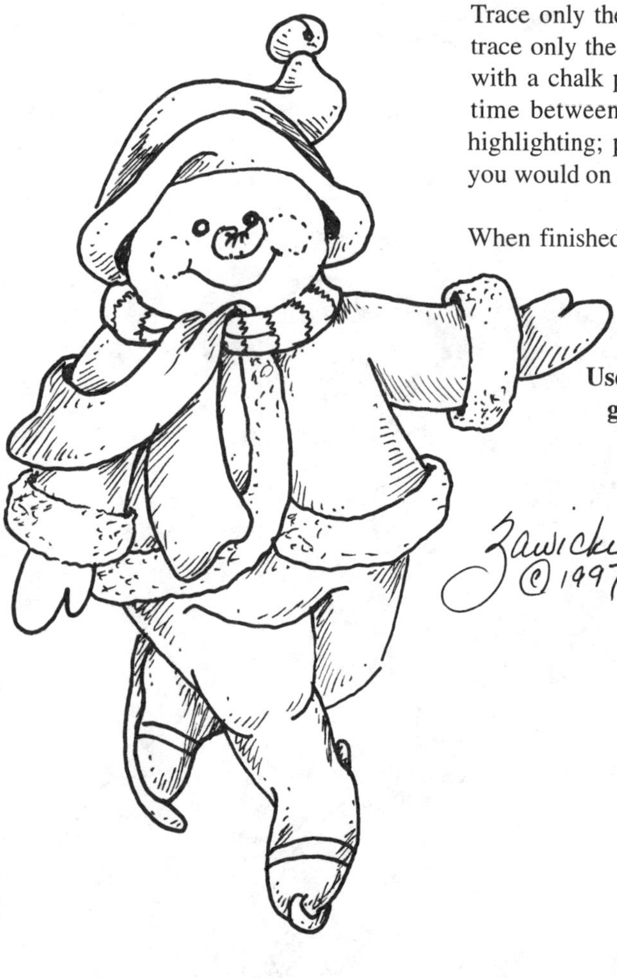

**Use these Santa Faces for the glass balls, using the nose of your choice.**

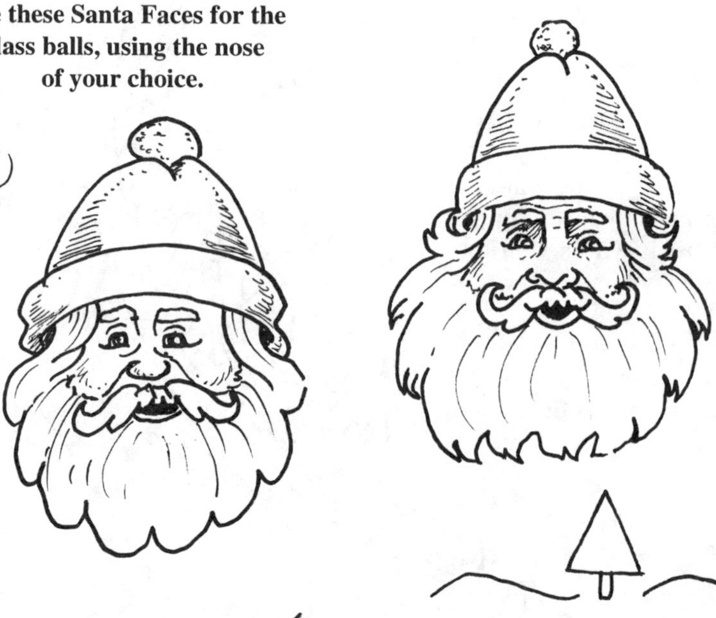

Zawicki ©1997

It's SNOW TIME!

# Misc. Strokework Designs Used on Small Pieces

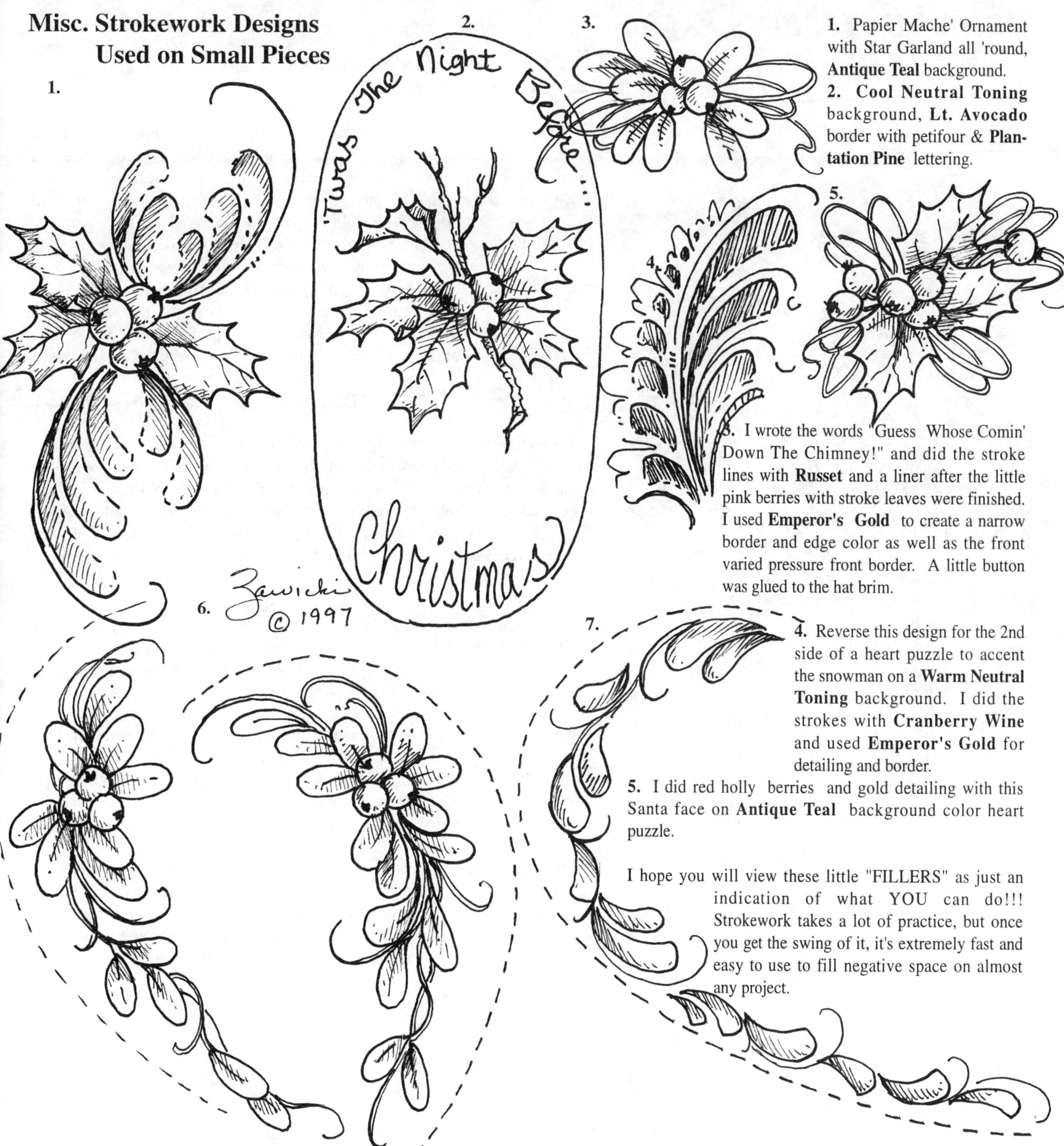


**1.** Papier Mache' Ornament with Star Garland all 'round, **Antique Teal** background.

**2. Cool Neutral Toning** background, **Lt. Avocado** border with petifour & **Plantation Pine** lettering.

**3.** I wrote the words "Guess Whose Comin' Down The Chimney!" and did the stroke lines with **Russet** and a liner after the little pink berries with stroke leaves were finished. I used **Emperor's Gold** to create a narrow border and edge color as well as the front varied pressure front border. A little button was glued to the hat brim.

**4.** Reverse this design for the 2nd side of a heart puzzle to accent the snowman on a **Warm Neutral Toning** background. I did the strokes with **Cranberry Wine** and used **Emperor's Gold** for detailing and border.

**5.** I did red holly berries and gold detailing with this Santa face on **Antique Teal** background color heart puzzle.

I hope you will view these little "FILLERS" as just an indication of what YOU can do!!! Strokework takes a lot of practice, but once you get the swing of it, it's extremely fast and easy to use to fill negative space on almost any project.

**6.** This design was done on a heart puzzle with **Cool Neutral Toning** background. Use regular leaf colors and perhaps **Charcoal Grey** line details for these projects. I use just a hint of shading with either **Charcoal, Midnite Green** or a brush-blend of both for shading the Winter Berries that are shaped with **Buttermilk** and highlighted with **Snow White**. A small red flush can also be added. Edge with gold.

**7. Russet** was used with **Mauve** for Santa's hat then carried over into both the stroke border and detailing over a **Warm Neutral Toning** background. Do a similar 2nd side. Monochromatic, but pretty. All of the these fillers have one thing in common. They use "c curve" strokes and opposing "c" curves in both the main strokes done with a flat shader, as well as those done with the liner brush. Line detail does not have to follow the exact lines of the strokes and can be interrupted.

# ORNAMENTS, PINS, & More!

*We all love painting AND receiving special Christmas ornaments and pins. The cute little canister (#37-033) comes from* **CABIN CRAFTERS**. *Reduce the skating snowman to make an adorable ornament too!*

Stain the canister your favorite shade. When dry, position the pattern and trace the outside of any portion that extends beyond the painted area. I used the **Antique Teal** for my background. It's such a neat dark background color! Use 1" masking tape to tape off the top and bottom of the straight lines. Bring tape right up to the traced design. By measuring in from the top or bottom and marking with a chalk pencil, you can make the borders any width you like. You will use floated color to background just the design areas that extend beyond the painted center. Fill in the rest of the area using a petifour sponge. It will probably require a couple of coats of background color. Trace with white graphite.

**THE CLOTHES:** A new hot color combo is aqua/teal, grey and red.
**Yellow Ochre** shaded with **Raw Sienna** for the hat tassel, skate strap and fur trim. Add a bit of darker shading on the fur with **Dark Chocolate.**
Float in the scarf, mittens, skate runners and inside hat fold-up with **Dove Grey** and shade with **Neutral Grey.** Float in the remainder of the hat and the jacket with **Warm Neutral Toning** creating a soft base that will keep the final red value, which is **Napa Red** shaded with a bit of **Cranberry Wine**.

**BASIC SANTA FACES:** *I'm afraid I find it hard to "give it a kiss", but these three fill the bill, with their simple shapes. It's to easy make them a little more realistic by making a more realistic nose and for one, the eyes. They definitely are a lot faster to paint if you're selling your work, as is.*

I used raw wood techniques for all three Santas. Use regular Santa face colors and simplify the eyes just a little. The nose is just a little floated button. Base in the beard & mustache with **Driftwood** then add the wispy white over that. The hats can be any color. I often float mine in with **Brandy Wine** over a WNT base. Use fine red ribbon or gold cord for ties.

Notice that all the ornaments in the book have been painted on a variety of different surfaces. Heart Puzzle cards, papier mache' ornaments, colored balls, boxes etc. Changing backgrounds and hat colors or adding a few little berries with leaves or strokework can make a whole new project, so just have fun! These are only a few ideas on using the designs!

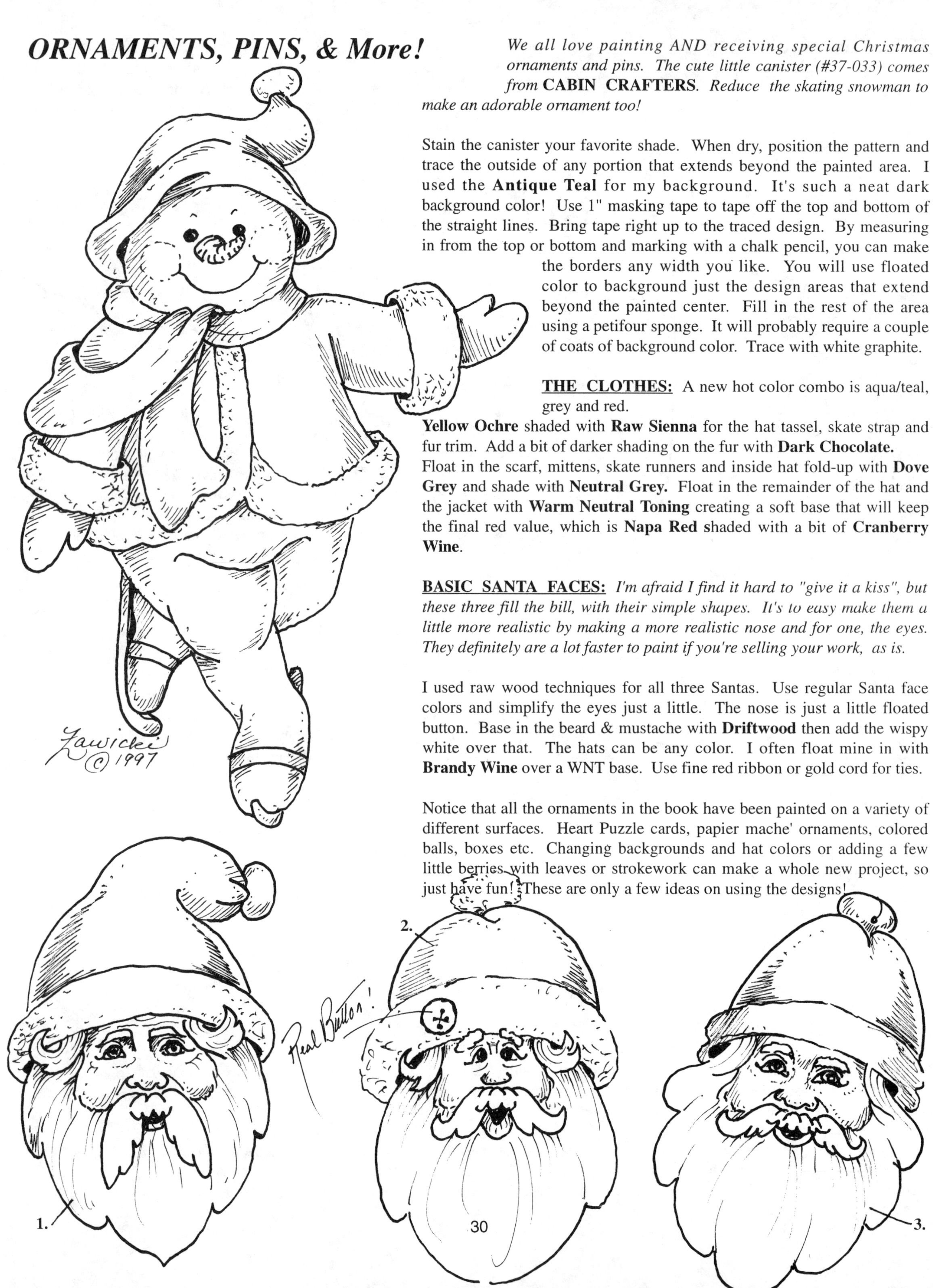

## MORE SANTA ORNAMENTS

*Here are a few more traditional little Santa faces. With so many Santa books behind me, it gets harder and harder to find new ideas for "Just faces". Refer to page 14 for face, beard and fur information. They were inspired by some favorites from the Santa ornament collection on my own tree. Why not send an ornament to someone special in an envelope or card. Sometimes we just can't get them cut from thin plywood as quickly as we'd like to get started painting. A painted ornament can be enjoyed for years to come, whether it is done on a puzzle heart, watercolor paper or as a thin wood cut-out!* **(Don't forget to paint the backs of ornaments too!)**

5.

4. I've done this one on the watercolor paper. Trace the design with very worn black graphite to get as light a line as possible and still be able to see it for watercolor paper. He would look great on a nice glass bottle too wouldn't he? I used **Cranberry Wine** for his hat. He is also done as a wood cut-out.

5. The original on this one was a wood carving. I enlarged the design to use it on the smallest **papier mache' star box** which was backgrounded with **Warm Neutral Toning** inside and out. Be sure that you add a little soft shading behind the side points so the show up more with a soft brush blend of **Russet + Charcoal Grey**. The points were outlined with a liner and **Emperor's Gold.** The hat was floated in with **Mauve** then shaded lightly with **Brandy Wine**. On the star box, I glued some sheer patterned paper onto the sides. It's a great way to decorate the box sides - and very little work! Instructions for application are included when ordering paper from us. We'll have several patterns available.

4.

6.

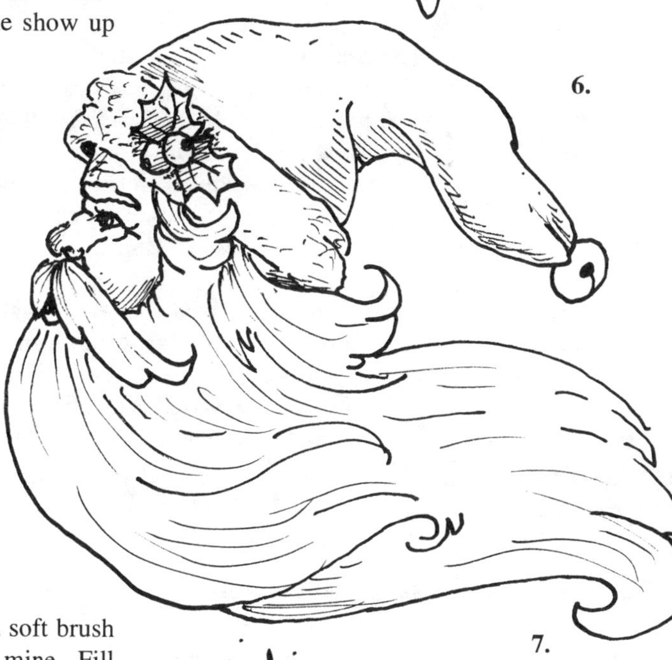

6. I chose to use this Santa on one of the lucite mugs from **Herr's, Inc.** and also as an ornament on watercolor paper. I did the hat **Napa Red.** I used a soft color when laying in the beard area. Be sure that you add a little soft shading behind the side points so the show up more. I used a soft brush blend of **Blue Haze + Midnite Green** for mine. Fill in with a little holly or some strokework. It was also done as a wood cut-out.

Jawicki ©1997

7.
**NOTE: I show a very simple back treatment too.**

7. I did the little star Santa on watercolor paper and as a wood cut-out. I used **Yellow Ochre** shaded with **Honey Brown** for the four yellow points. Highlight with **Taffy Cream**. The hat was washed with the Golden Straw, then floated with **Brandy Wine.** Use beard colors for the hat tassel. Write a message on the back.

<u>**Worried about losing the pattern?**</u> I've shown a raw wood cut-out with a "found face" Trace with white graphite, then outline the eyes and mouth interior with **Charcoal Grey**. Outline the nose first, centering it beneath the bridge of the nose, the bottom of the lip-line and the sides of the face with **Shading Flesh** and the brows & mustache with **Neutral Grey.** Thin paint for a very fine line. **Also, the curve makes it hard to trace onto a round ornament. Make it easier by tracing only the face or main part, then free-handing the beards, hats, etc.**

## PATTERN PACKETS

Jean has designed numerous otherwise unpublished pattern packets ranging in price from $3.50 to $7.00. It is our firm policy NEVER to include packet projects in book publications. Due to popular demand, my packets have leaned heavily toward St. Nick, although I have a series of small decorator furniture packets and a few other miscellaneous subjects. Each contains complete written instructions, detailed line drawings and one or more color photographs.

**Send a double-stamped, business size self-addressed envelope + $2 (refundable with first order) to receive your copy.**

## PAINTING BORDERS

It's a lot easier to get your border stroke pattern more even by doing all "like" portions all the way around the entire area.

**EXAMPLE: Small Russet plate border used for the reduced design on page13.**

Using the curve of the plate, I drew in the curved lines with a fine liner. Be sure that you create a little tear shape at each end. Next I did the left side teardrop strokes all around, following with the strokes on the right side. Try to make each individual stroke as like all others as you can. I then did the grids in on direction all around, then the other direction. Last I added random dip-dots with a stylus. All was done with a liner and **Emperor's Gold** acrylic.

No matter what border you choose to create, you will always get a better balance if you do the work piece by piece as opposed to working one whole section at a time to completion. You can also use a ruler and chalk pencil to measure and mark spaces more evenly if you wish. Use varied pressure with either a liner or a small flat shader to create curved or square angled borders also.

Have Fun!

**Herr's Inc.** *
70 Eastgate Dr.
Danville, Il 61834
**(800) 637-2647**

**Wayne's Woodenware** **
1913 State Road 150
Neenah, WI 54956
**(414) 725-7986**

**Viking Woodcraft, Inc.** *
1318 8th Street SE
Waseca, MN 56093
**(507) 835-1898**
**(Viking carries many products used)**

**CABIN CRAFTERS** **
Jeff and Sherry Foster
1225 W. First St. (P.O. Box 270)
Nevada, IA 50201

**Zim's Inc.** *
4370 Commerce Dr.
Salt Lake City, UT 84107
**(801) 268-2505**
(800) 669-3920

*** Wholesale Only**
**** Wholesale & Retail**

**We also stock many of these products in our shop and can ship if you are unable to find these or similar products in your own area.**

## BOOKS by JEAN ZAWICKI

**Many older book publications are still available through the authors, even though distributors have discontinued stocking them. We ship UPS daily.**

| | |
|---|---|
| *JEAN FLIPS FOR GIFTS * | 6.50 |
| **NATURE'S TREASURES 2* | 7.95 |
| COUNTRY QUILTIN' | 9.50 |
| COLLECTOR'S CHRISTMAS | 9.95 |
| DECORATIVE TOUCHES | 9.95 |
| BRIARHILL BUNNY | 9.95 |
| COBWEBS & CHRISTMAS | 8.95 |
| SANTA & ME Vol. 2 | 8.95 |
| HEIRLOOM SANTAS | 9.95 |

**One** * before a title instructions written for oil only.
**Two** ** before title oil & acrylic projects
**No** * indicates that the book is totally written for acrylic.
*** after the title** indicates that the book is in **very limited** supply.

Check at your local tole shop for Jean's books first, or order directly from Zawicki Publications. **Include $3.50 to help cover the cost of shipping. WI. residents** please include **5 1/2%** state sales tax.

**Dealer Inquiries Welcome**

Many of the pieces in the book are original pieces of my own design. Viking often offers many of the new wood pieces for the wholesale market. I've also given the source for some of the other pieces that I've used.
We try to keep especially the small cut-outs and some other wood pieces in stock in our shop supply room, but our space is limited. I can order things for you if you're unable to order wholesale or can't find them in your own area. **UPS** picks up daily. Refer to the shipping costs at left for written material, then **Please add 10% to the total amount due on any wood or items other than written materials.** Call in your orders with Visa or Mastercard for immediate shipment and we'll use exact shipping charges.

**HEART PUZZLES** 6 (w/envelopes) $5.00
**ORNAMENT CUT-OUTS** - $1 ea. (Please order by page and the design numbers given next to the designs )
**Thin DOOR HANGERS** $1.00 each
**Painter's Pal Sta-Wet** palette- $16.95 Refill paper $5.95
**Stick Erasers** - $1.10 ea. **Chalk Pencils** - $1.00 each
**1/4" Filbert Rake** - $11.79 **1/2" Fil. Rake** - $15.59
**Dry-It Boards** - 9x12", $8.95 and 12x15, $10.95
**Tic-Tac-Toe Boards** - $7.50 each
**Tic-Tac-Toe Snowman & Tree Playing Pieces** - 60¢ each
**Snow-Tex -** 2 oz. $1.69 and 4 oz. $3.49
**Glamour Dust -** 29.5g $4.49
**MAGNA-TAC GLUE** - 8 oz. bottle $6.95 **NOTE:** This is truly the **BEST glue** I've ever used, however it's not easy to find!